# Beanstalk's Basics for PIANO
## THEORY BOOK
## LEVEL 1

### BY CHERYL FINN

To access stickers, visit:
**www.halleonard.com/mylibrary**

Enter Code
5113-8454-7167-5274

ISBN 978-0-87718-045-6

EXCLUSIVELY DISTRIBUTED BY
HAL•LEONARD®
—A Muse Group Company—

© 2000 by The Willis Music Co.
International Copyright Secured  All Rights Reserved

No part of this publication may be reproduced in any form or by
any means without the prior written permission of the Publisher.

Visit Hal Leonard Online at
**www.halleonard.com**

World headquarters, contact:
**Hal Leonard**
7777 West Bluemound Road
Milwaukee, WI 53213
Email: info@halleonard.com

In Europe, contact:
**Hal Leonard Europe Limited**
Dettingen Way
Bury St Edmunds, Suffolk, IP33 3YB
Email: info@halleonardeurope.com

In Australia, contact:
**Hal Leonard Australia Pty. Ltd.**
4 Lentara Court
Cheltenham, Victoria, 3192 Australia
Email: info@halleonard.com.au

# CONTENTS

| | |
|---|---|
| Note Review | 3 |
| Dynamic Sign Review | 3 |
| Interval Review ---- Melodic 2nds & 3rds | 4 |
| Slur Review | 4 |
| Interval Review ---- Harmonic 2nds & 3rds | 5 |
| Counting | 5 |
| Interval Review ---- 4ths & 5ths | 6 |
| Dynamic Sign Review | 6 |
| Staccato Review | 7 |
| Triads | 8 |
| Puzzle Fun! | 9 |
| Note Review | 10 |
| Note Writing | 10 |
| Reviewing Accidentals: Sharp (♯) | 11 |
| Reviewing Accidentals: Flat (♭) | 12 |
| A New Dynamic Sign: mezzo forte ( *mf* ) | 12 |
| Note Review | 13 |
| Note Naming | 13 |
| G Position Triad | 13 |
| Slur & Tie Review | 14 |
| A New Dynamic Sign: mezzo piano ( *mp* ) | 14 |
| Review | 15 |
| Eighth Notes (♫) | 17 |
| Fermata ( ⌢ ) | 18 |
| Counting With Eighth Notes | 18 |
| Adding Bar Lines | 19 |
| Accents ( > ) | 20 |
| Notes and Stems | 20 |
| Note Review | 21 |
| Note Naming | 21 |
| More Notes & Stems | 22 |
| Adding Bar Lines | 22 |
| F Position Triad | 23 |
| Secret Melody! | 23 |
| Note Writing | 24 |
| D Position Triad | 25 |
| Puzzle Fun! (Tic-Tac-Toe) | 25 |
| Riddles! | 26 |
| Counting & Bar Lines | 27 |
| Note Naming | 28 |
| A New G Position Triad | 29 |
| Triad Review | 29 |
| Review | 30 |
| Key Signatures | 32 |
| More Key Signatures! | 33 |
| Sharps (♯) | 34 |
| Flats (♭) | 35 |
| How's Your Italian? | 36 |
| Compose It! | 37 |
| Octave Higher (8$^{va}$ - - - ⌐) | 38 |
| Octave Lower (8$^{va}$ - - - ⌐) | 39 |
| Secret Melody! | 40 |
| Riddles! | 41 |
| Note Naming | 42 |
| Puzzle Fun! You Be The Teacher! | 43 |
| Counting & Bar Lines | 44 |
| Naturals ( ♮ ) | 45 |
| Note Writing | 46 |
| Review | 47 |

# A NOTE TO PARENTS AND TEACHERS

The study of music theory is essential to the development of the young musician. Not only does this study help to expand upon the concepts taught at the piano lesson, but it also gives the student a greater understanding and appreciation of the wonder that is music.

The Beanstalk series was designed to be used with colorful, attractive stickers that reward a job well done. The student may receive stickers for note-naming and note-writing drills, for ear training, and sight-reading exercises, and for successfully completing review pages. These exclusive stickers are available for download using the unique code found on the title page of this book and may be printed using Avery Round Labels (6450), available at Avery.com and other online retailers.

Each theory page corresponds directly with material covered in **Beanstalk's Basics for Piano.** The student progresses gradually, in a logical fashion and continually builds on concepts previously learned.

**Beanstalk's Basics for Piano Theory** also features a further learning tool called **Thinking Cap. Thinking Cap** challenges the student to search for answers to one or more theoretical questions and to provide these answers verbally as part of a musical dialogue. This fun exercise encourages students to carefully consider and discuss new concepts as they arise.

We wish much success to all students as they strive to expand their musical horizons!

*To Alanna and Brianne*

# NOTE REVIEW

**C POSITION**

Name the following whole notes in the **TREBLE CLEF**.

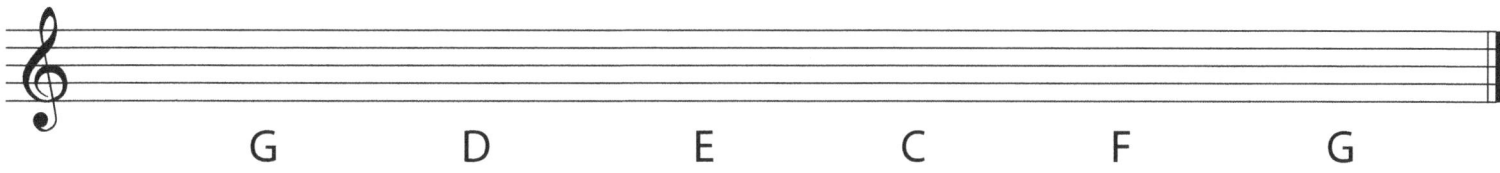

___  ___  ___  ___  ___  ___

Write the following notes on the **TREBLE** staff. Use whole notes.

G   D   E   C   F   G

Name the following whole notes in the **BASS CLEF**.

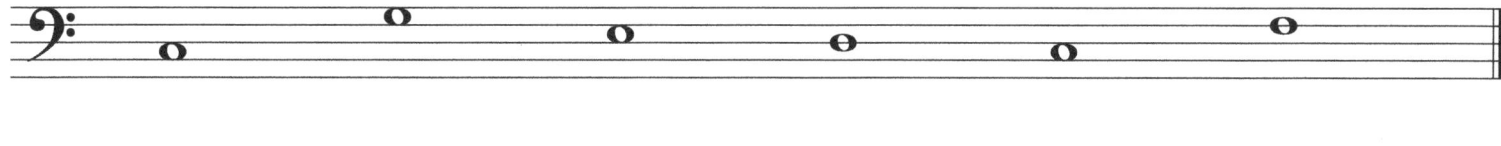

___  ___  ___  ___  ___  ___

Write the following notes on the **BASS** staff. Use whole notes.

G   C   D   F   G   E

# DYNAMIC SIGN REVIEW

1. Draw a sign which tells us to play **LOUDLY**. _____

2. Draw a sign which tells us to play **GRADUALLY SOFTER**. _____

CORRESPONDS WITH PAGE 4 OF BEANSTALK'S LESSON BOOK 1.

# INTERVAL REVIEW
# MELODIC 2NDS & 3RDS

An **INTERVAL** is the distance between **TWO** notes.

A **MELODIC** interval occurs between two notes which are written and played **SEPARATELY**.

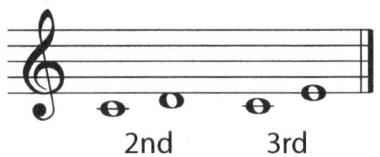

For each of the following, draw a whole note which is a **MELODIC 2ND** above.

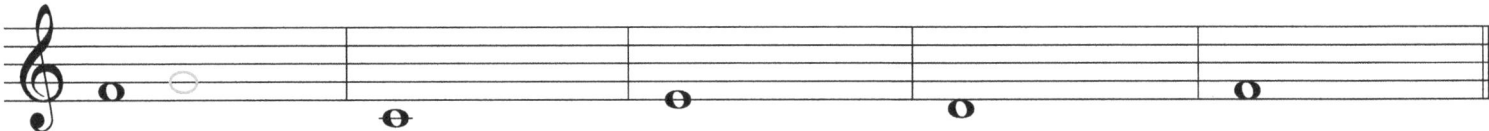

For each of the following, draw a whole note which is a **MELODIC 3RD** above.

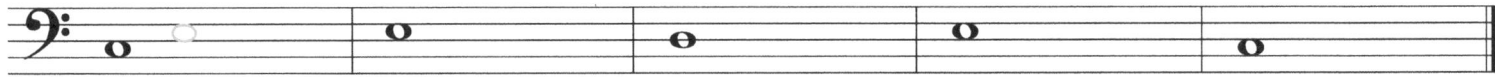

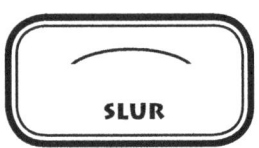

# SLUR REVIEW

A **SLUR** tells us to play the notes **SMOOTHLY CONNECTED** or **LEGATO**. Longer slurs are called phrase lines.

1. Draw a **SLUR** to connect each group of **FOUR** notes.
2. Sight read the melody.
3. Name the notes.

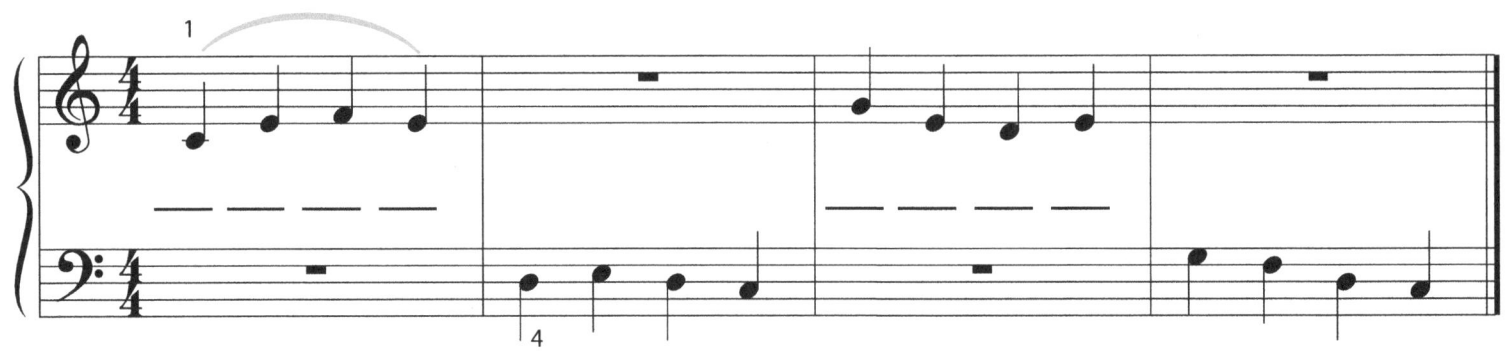

**NOW HEAR THIS!**

Your teacher will play a series of **MELODIC 2nds** and **3rds**. Close your eyes and listen. Are the **2nds** and **3rds** going **UP** or **DOWN**?

**FOR THE TEACHER:**

CORRESPONDS WITH PAGE 5 OF BEANSTALK'S LESSON BOOK 1.

# INTERVAL REVIEW
# HARMONIC 2NDS & 3RDS

An **HARMONIC** interval occurs between two notes which are written and played **TOGETHER**.

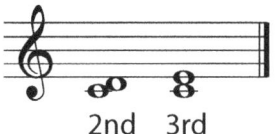

For each of the following, draw a whole note which is an **HARMONIC 2ND** above.

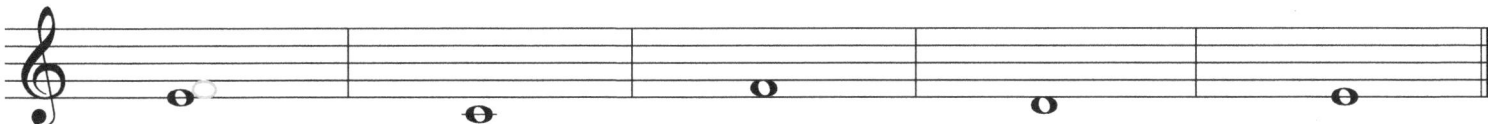

For each of the following, draw a whole note which is an **HARMONIC 3RD** above.

**NOW HEAR THIS!**

Your teacher will play a series of **2nds** and **3rds**. Close your eyes and listen. Are the intervals **HARMONIC** or **MELODIC**?

**FOR THE TEACHER:**

# COUNTING

Write the counts for the following. Remember to check the time signature!

1 2 3 4

CORRESPONDS WITH PAGE 6 OF BEANSTALK'S LESSON BOOK 1.

# INTERVAL REVIEW
# 4THS & 5THS

**THINKING CAP**
How can you tell if an interval is *HARMONIC* or *MELODIC*?

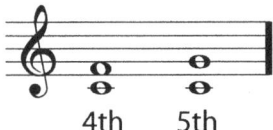
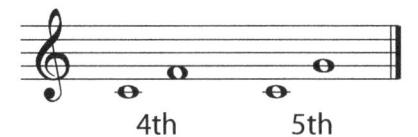

Are the following **HARMONIC** intervals *4ths* or *5ths*?

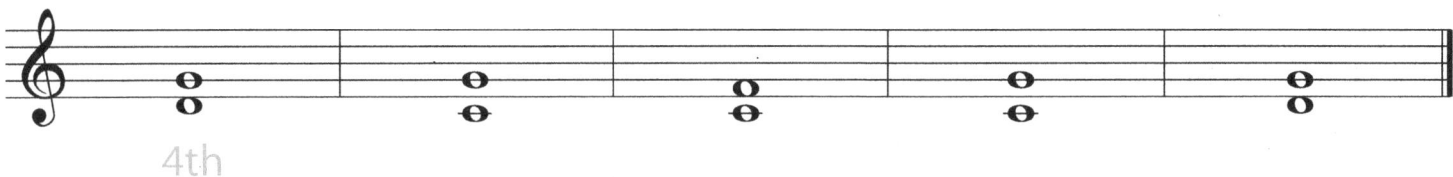

4th   _____   _____   _____   _____

Are the following **MELODIC** intervals *4ths* or *5ths*?

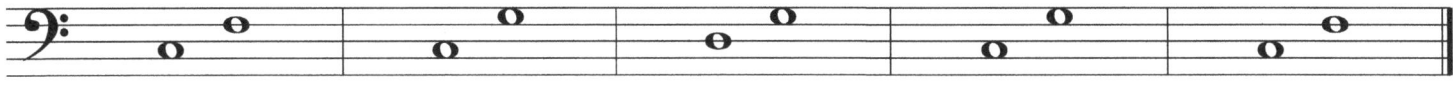

_____   _____   _____   _____   _____

Add a note above to complete each of the following **HARMONIC** intervals. Use whole notes.

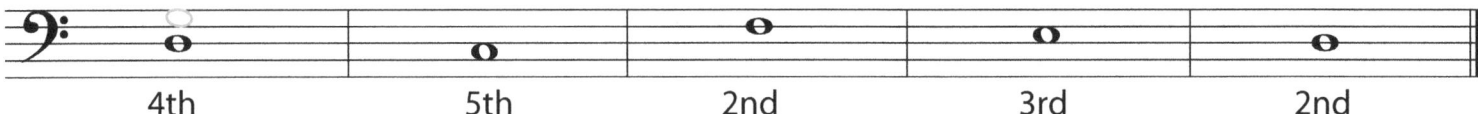

4th        5th        2nd        3rd        2nd

Add a note above to complete each of the following **MELODIC** intervals. Use whole notes.

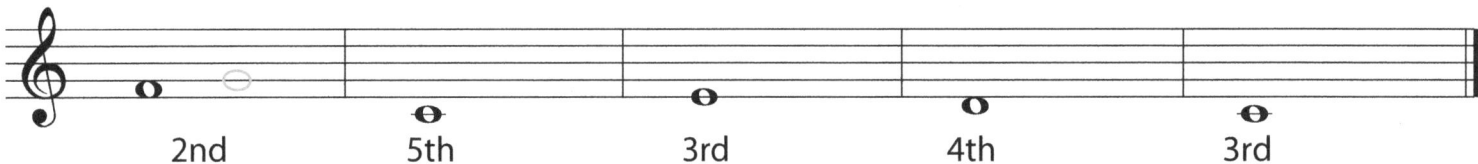

2nd        5th        3rd        4th        3rd

# DYNAMIC SIGN REVIEW

Draw a sign which tells us to play **SOFTLY**. _____

Draw a sign which tells us to play **GRADUALLY LOUDER**. _____

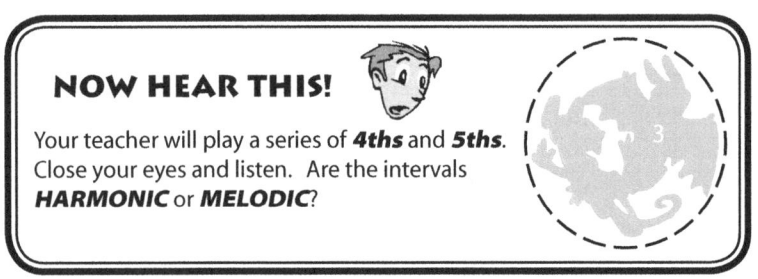

**NOW HEAR THIS!**
Your teacher will play a series of *4ths* and *5ths*. Close your eyes and listen. Are the intervals *HARMONIC* or *MELODIC*?

CORRESPONDS WITH PAGES 7 & 8 OF BEANSTALK'S LESSON BOOK 1.

# STACCATO REVIEW

**STACCATO** tells us to play **DETACHED** or **CRISPLY**.

**REMEMBER:** If the note stem goes **UP** ( ) the dot goes **BELOW** the note. If the note stem goes **DOWN** ( ) the dot goes **ABOVE** the note.

1. Add **STACCATO DOTS** above or below the following notes.
2. Sight read the melody.
3. What does this piece sound like to you? (Make up a title!)
4. Name the notes.

_____
(Title)

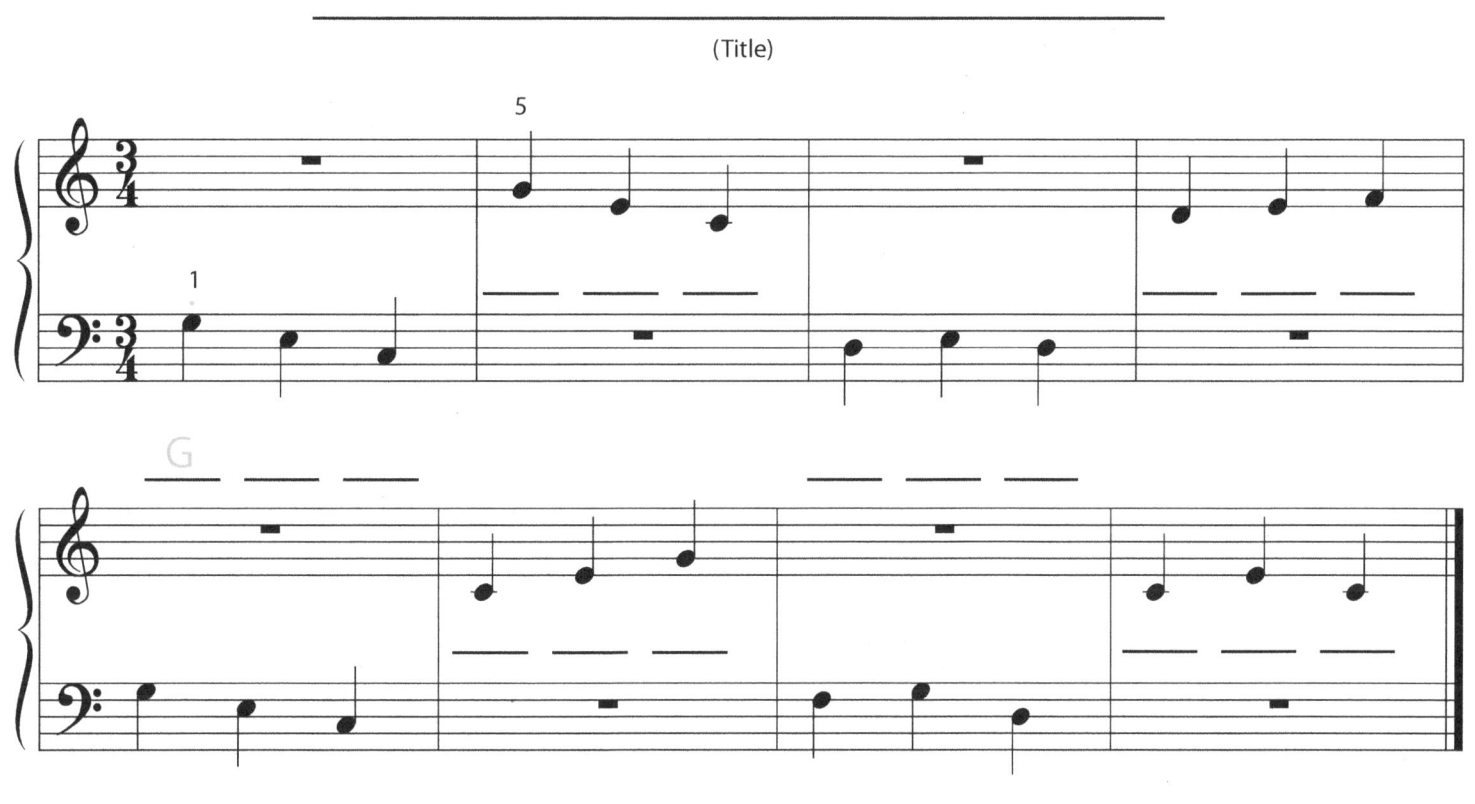

**NOW HEAR THIS!**

Your teacher will play a series of notes. Close your eyes and listen. Are the notes you are hearing played **STACCATO** or **LEGATO**?

CORRESPONDS WITH PAGE 9 OF BEANSTALK'S LESSON BOOK 1.

# TRIADS

A **CHORD** is a group of notes played together at the same time.

A **TRIAD** is a **THREE-NOTE CHORD**. Each note is written a 3rd above:

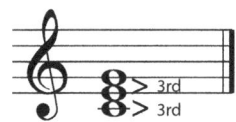 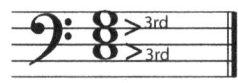

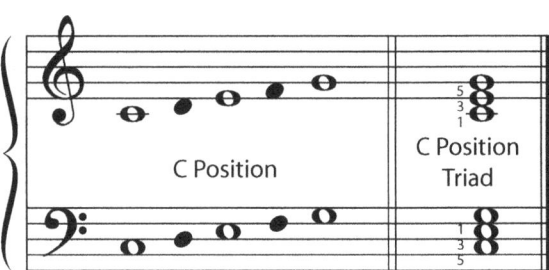

Practice writing **C POSITION TRIADS** below. Remember if the triad begins on a **LINE** note, the notes above it will also be **LINE** notes. If the triad begins on a **SPACE** note, the notes above it will also be **SPACE** notes. (We call this a **C POSITION TRIAD** because it begins on **C**.)

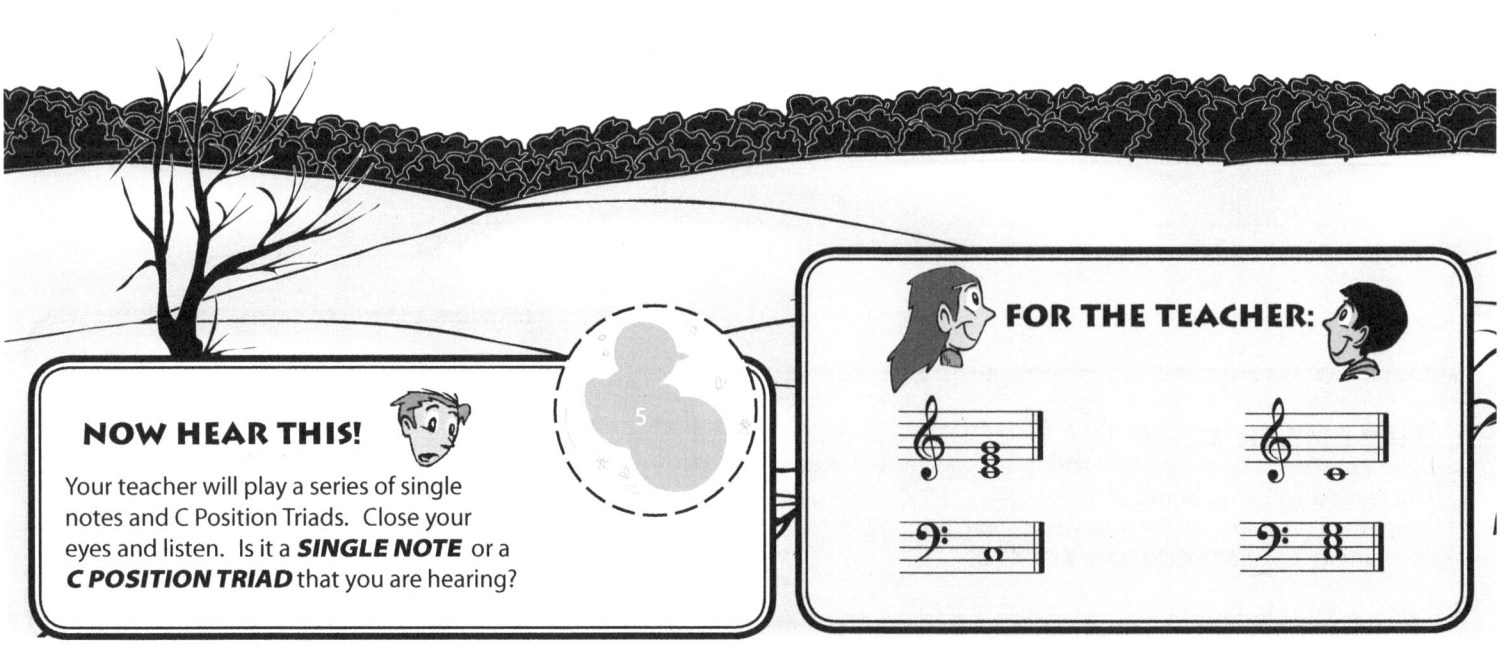

### NOW HEAR THIS!

Your teacher will play a series of single notes and C Position Triads. Close your eyes and listen. Is it a **SINGLE NOTE** or a **C POSITION TRIAD** that you are hearing?

**FOR THE TEACHER:**

CORRESPONDS WITH PAGE 10 OF BEANSTALK'S LESSON BOOK 1.

# PUZZLE FUN!

1. Find the opposites! Draw a line to connect each sign to its opposite meaning.

2. Use the clues on the right to find the missing letters below.

**WORD HELPER BOX**

FORTE
CRESCENDO
SLUR
CHORD
PIANO
STACCATO
DECRESCENDO
TRIAD

**CLUES**

1. SOFT
2. SMOOTHLY
3. CRISPLY OR DETACHED
4. A GROUP OF NOTES PLAYED AT THE SAME TIME
5. LOUD
6. A THREE-NOTE CHORD
7. GRADUALLY GETTING LOUDER
8. GRADUALLY GETTING SOFTER

3. Write the numbered letters below to find out what's **FUN**!

\_\_\_ \_\_\_ \_\_\_ \_\_\_ \_\_\_ \_\_\_ \_\_\_ \_\_\_ **is FUN!**
 1   2   3   4   5   6   7   8

CORRESPONDS WITH PAGE 11 OF BEANSTALK'S LESSON BOOK 1.

# NOTE REVIEW

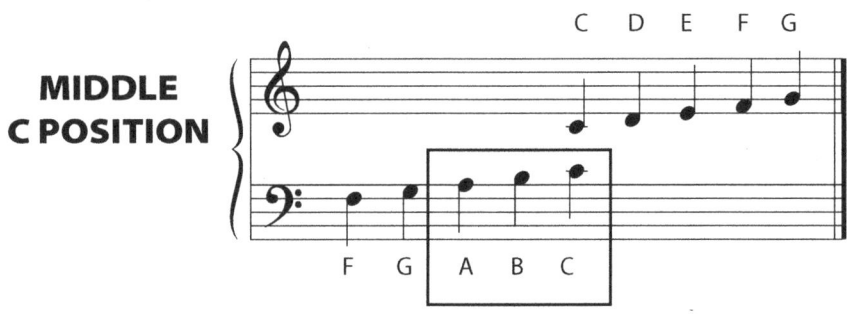

MIDDLE C POSITION

# NOTE WRITING

Time yourself writing the following whole notes.
(Remember to check the clef!)

E  D  C  C  E  F  D

B  F  G  F  A  C  B

C  E  F  D  C  E  F

A  C  G  F  B  F  A

I wrote these notes in _____ minutes and _____ seconds!

CORRESPONDS WITH PAGES 12 & 13 OF BEANSTALK'S LESSON BOOK 1.

# REVIEWING ACCIDENTALS

A **SHARP** sign tells us to play the closest key to the **RIGHT**. When we write a sharp sign, we place it **IN FRONT** of the note: ♯o

**REMEMBER:** If the sharp sign is in front of a **SPACE** note, the sharp sign must go in the **SPACE**.

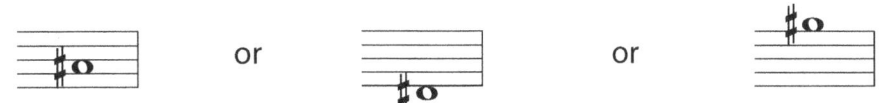

Practice writing a **SHARP** sign in front of these **SPACE** notes. Name the notes.

**THINKING CAP**
Will a sharp sign go on a **LINE** or in a **SPACE** if the note is a middle C?

**REMEMBER:** If the sharp sign is in front of a **LINE** note, the sharp sign must go on the **LINE**.

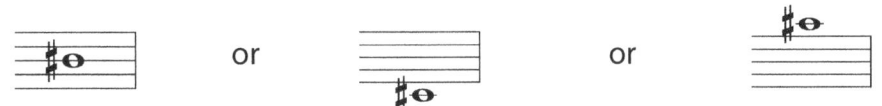

Practice writing a **SHARP** sign in front of these **LINE** notes. Name the notes.

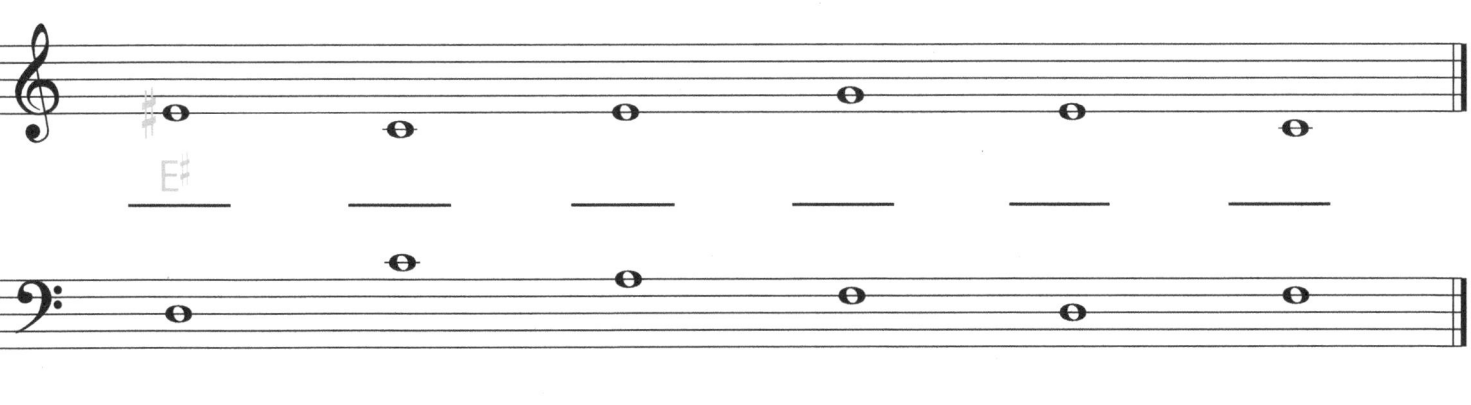

CORRESPONDS WITH PAGE 14 OF BEANSTALK'S LESSON BOOK 1.

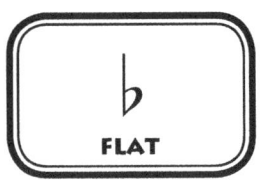

# REVIEWING ACCIDENTALS

A **FLAT** sign tells us to play the closest key to the **LEFT**. When we write a flat sign, we place it **IN FRONT** of the note: ♭o

**REMEMBER:** If the flat sign is in front of a **SPACE** note, the flat sign must go in the **SPACE**.

Practice writing a **FLAT** sign in front of these **SPACE** notes. Name the notes.

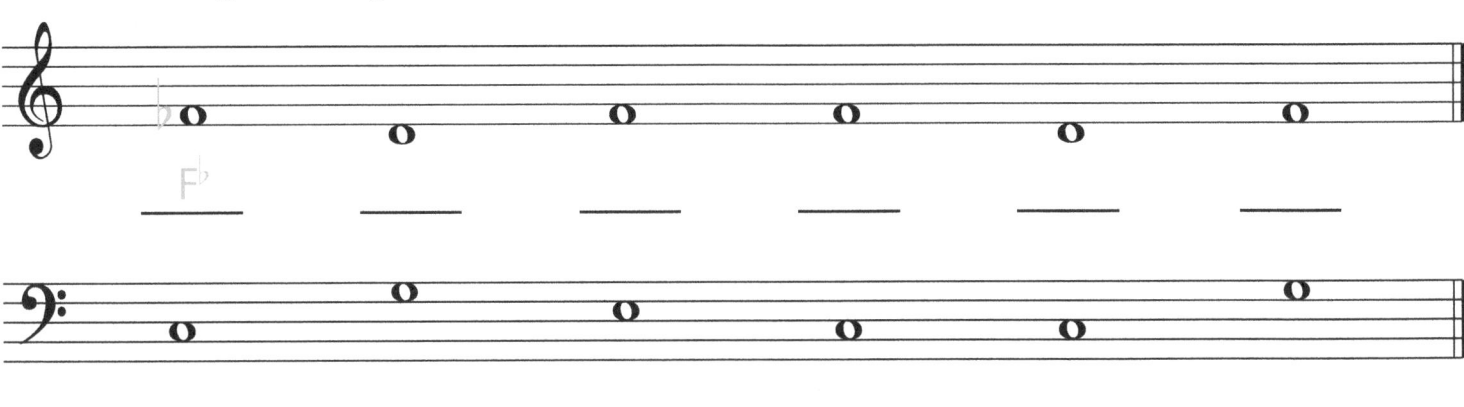

**REMEMBER:** If the flat sign is in front of a **LINE** note, the flat sign must go on the **LINE**.

**THINKING CAP**
Will a flat sign go on a **LINE** or in a **SPACE** if the note is on a line?

Practice writing a **FLAT** sign in front of these **LINE** notes. Name the notes.

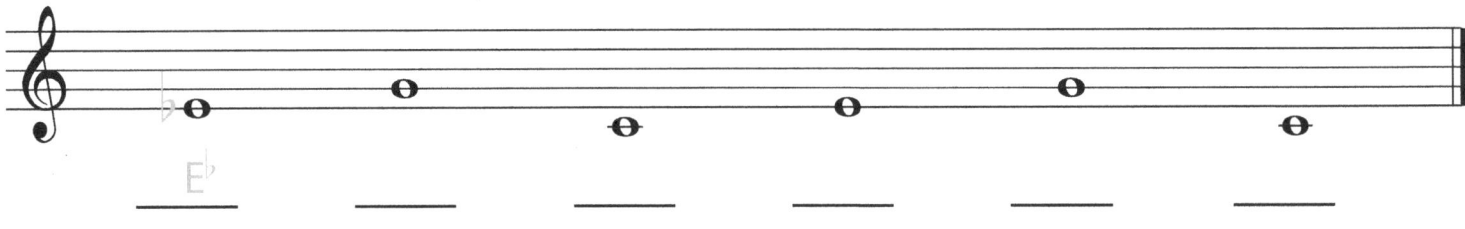

# A NEW DYNAMIC SIGN

Write **FOUR** more **MEZZO FORTE** signs.

**MEZZO FORTE** means to play moderately loud.

CORRESPONDS WITH PAGE 15 OF BEANSTALK'S LESSON BOOK 1.

# NOTE REVIEW

**G POSITION**

# NOTE NAMING

Time yourself naming the following notes on the grand staff. Be sure to check whether the notes are written in the **TREBLE CLEF** or the **BASS CLEF**.

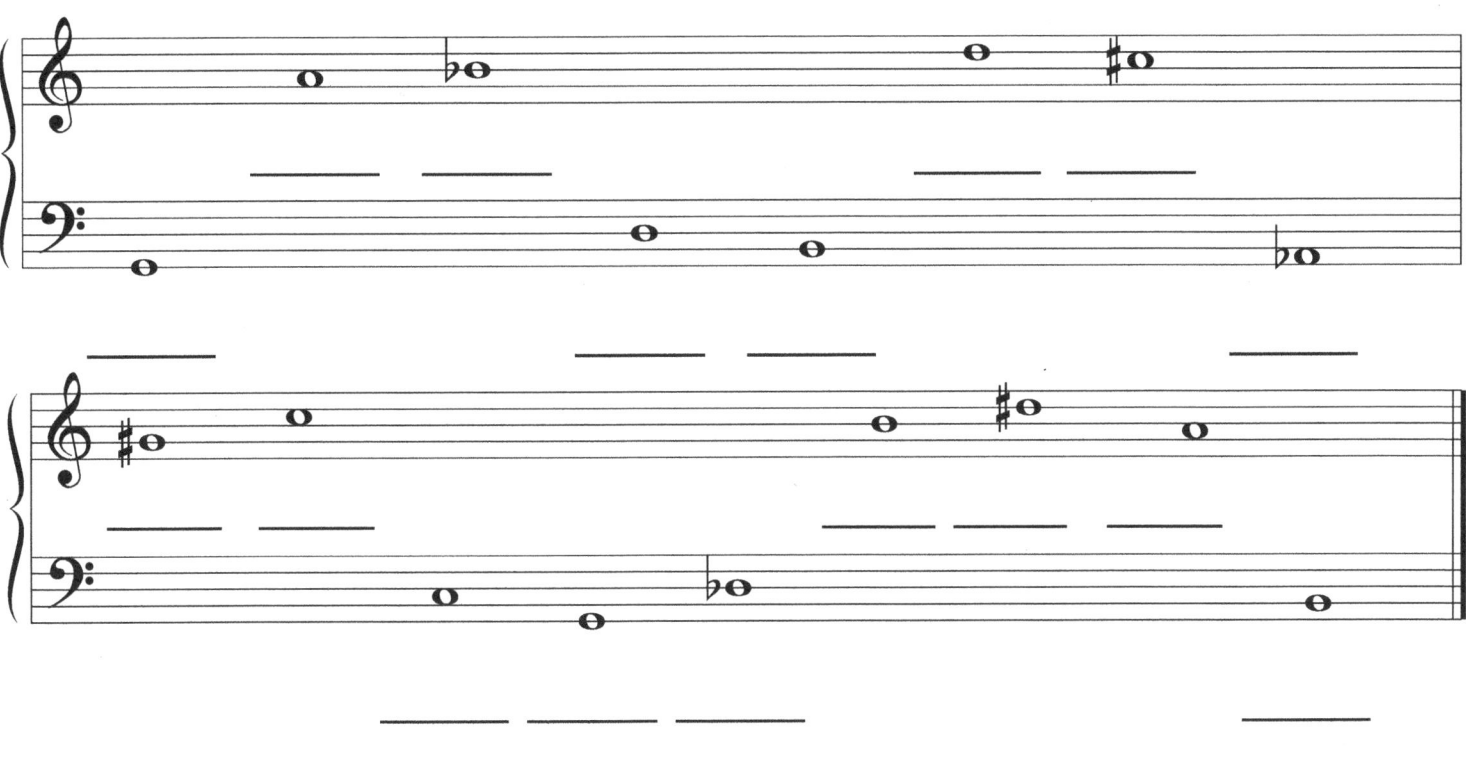

I named these notes in _____ minutes and _____ seconds!

# G POSITION TRIAD

Practice writing **G POSITION TRIADS** below.

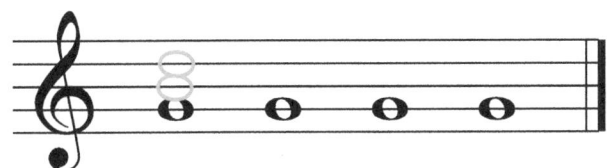

CORRESPONDS WITH PAGE 16 OF BEANSTALK'S LESSON BOOK 1.

13

# SLUR & TIE REVIEW

A **SLUR** and a **TIE** may look very similar, but their meanings are completely different! A **SLUR** tells us to play **SMOOTHLY**, while a **TIE** between two notes tells us to **HOLD** for the value of **BOTH** notes. Do you remember how to tell these signs apart?

**REMEMBER:** If the notes are **DIFFERENT**, it is a **SLUR**:

If the notes are the **SAME**, it is a **TIE**:

For each of the melodies below, draw a **CIRCLE** around all of the **SLURS**.

Put a **BOX** around all of the **TIES**.

Add up the total number of **TIES** and the total number of **SLURS**. Record your answers below. Who is the winner?

Total number of **SLURS** is _____ . Total number of **TIES** is _____ . The winner is _____ !

# A NEW DYNAMIC SIGN

**MEZZO PIANO** means to play moderately soft.

Write **FOUR** more **MEZZO PIANO** signs.

*mp* _____

CORRESPONDS WITH PAGE 17 OF BEANSTALK'S LESSON BOOK 1.

# REVIEW

1. Name the following whole notes on the grand staff.

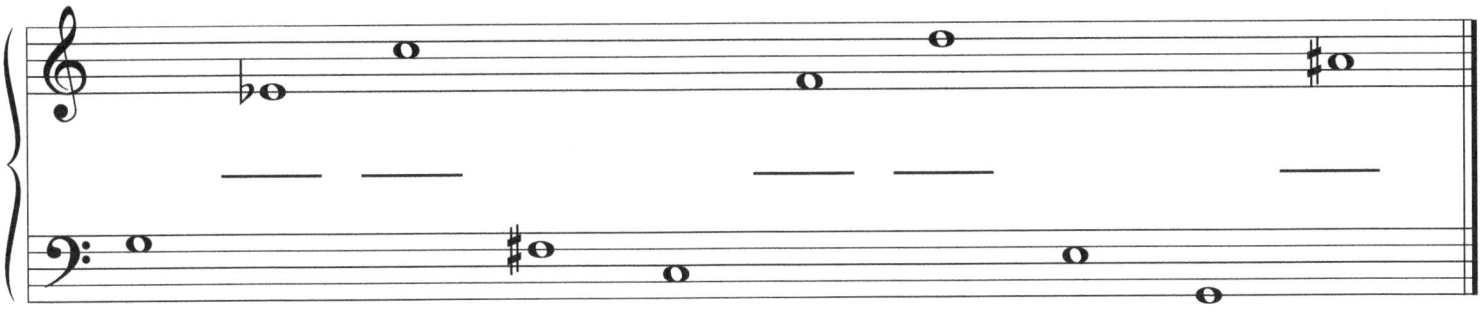

2. Write the following notes on the grand staff. Use whole notes.

3. Write the following **TRIADS**. Remember to check the clef!

C Position Triad     G Position Triad     C Position Triad     G Position Triad

4. Write the counts to the following. Clap the rhythm and count out loud.

CORRESPONDS WITH PAGE 18 OF BEANSTALK'S LESSON BOOK 1.

5. Add a note above to complete the following **HARMONIC** intervals. Use whole notes.

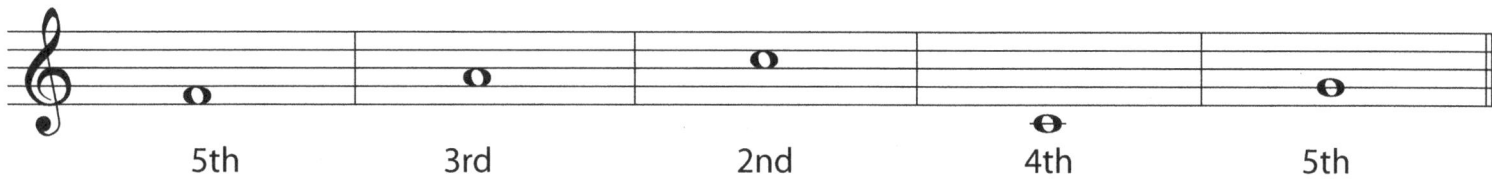

6. Add a note above to complete the following **MELODIC** intervals. Use whole notes.

7. Put a **CIRCLE** around the **SLURS** and a **BOX** around the **TIES**.

8. Draw the dynamic sign for each of the following.

**MODERATELY LOUD** _____

**LOUD** _____

**SOFT** _____

**GRADUALLY SOFTER** _____

**MODERATELY SOFT** _____

**GRADUALLY LOUDER** _____

CORRESPONDS WITH PAGE 18 OF BEANSTALK'S LESSON BOOK 1.

# EIGHTH NOTES

This is a single **EIGHTH NOTE**: stem up → ♪  ♪ ← stem down

Let's trace and fill in, stems up. →

Let's trace and fill in, stems down. →

Draw 8 more single eighth notes, stems up.

Draw 8 more single eighth notes, stems down.

**EIGHTH NOTES** are often grouped in **TWOS**: Beam ↘ ♫ or ♫ ← Beam
**TWO EIGHTH NOTES** joined together are equal in time to **ONE QUARTER NOTE** which we count "one and" or "1 +".   ♫ or ♫    ♫ = ♩
one and   1 +

Let's trace and fill in, stems up.

count:  1  +  1  +  1  +  1  +

Let's trace and fill in, stems down.

count:  1  +  1  +  1  +  1  +

Draw two pairs of eighth notes with stems going **UP**, and two pairs with stems going **DOWN**.

CORRESPONDS WITH PAGE 19 OF BEANSTALK'S LESSON BOOK 1.

# FERMATA

A **FERMATA** or **PAUSE** means that the note is to be **HELD LONGER** than its usual value.

Trace these **FERMATA** signs.

Draw six more **FERMATA** signs.

# COUNTING WITH EIGHTH NOTES

Write counts for the following measures. Clap the rhythm and count out loud.

1  2  3    1  2  3    1  2  3    1  2  3

### NOW HEAR THIS!
Your teacher will play a series of short melodies containing eighth notes. Close your eyes and listen. After having heard the melody played twice, clap the rhythm.

### FOR THE TEACHER:

CORRESPONDS WITH PAGES 20 & 21 OF BEANSTALK'S LESSON BOOK 1.

# ADDING BAR LINES

**BAR LINES** divide the music into equal measures or bars. To find the number of counts needed for each measure, look at the time signature. The top number tells you how many counts you will need. For example, if the time signature is 3/4, you will need 3 counts in each measure.

First put counts under the notes until you have enough counts for a measure, then draw your first bar line. Continue in the same way until all of the bar lines are in their proper positions.

For example:

Write the counts and add bar lines to the following. Clap the rhythm and count out loud.

CORRESPONDS WITH PAGE 22 OF BEANSTALK'S LESSON BOOK 1

# ACCENTS

An **ACCENT** sign placed **ABOVE** or **BELOW** a note means that the note is to be played **LOUDER** than usual.

Trace these **ACCENT** signs. (**NOTE**: when the note stem goes **UP**, the accent sign goes **BELOW** the note. When the note stem goes **DOWN**, the accent sign goes **ABOVE** the note.)

Draw **ACCENT** signs **ABOVE** or **BELOW** these notes.

# NOTES & STEMS

**THINKING CAP**
What is the difference between a **FERMATA** and an **ACCENT** sign?

When adding stems to notes remember these rules:

If the note is **BELOW** the middle line, the stem goes **UP**:

If the note is **ABOVE** the middle line, the stem goes **DOWN**:

If the note is **ON** the middle line, the stem can go **UP** or **DOWN**:

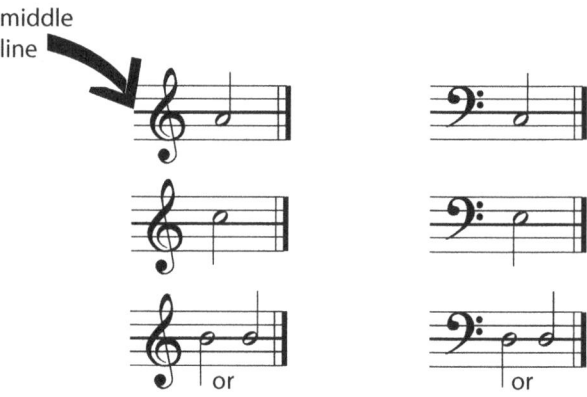

Add stems to the following note heads. (Notice how they will become half notes!) Name the notes.

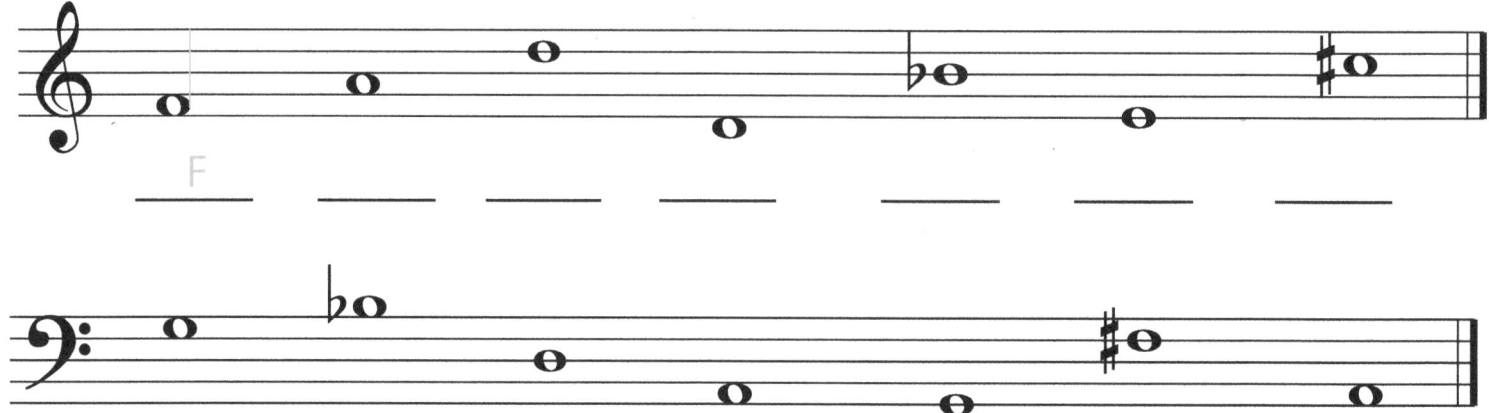

CORRESPONDS WITH PAGE 23 OF BEANSTALK'S LESSON BOOK 1.

# NOTE REVIEW

**F POSITION**

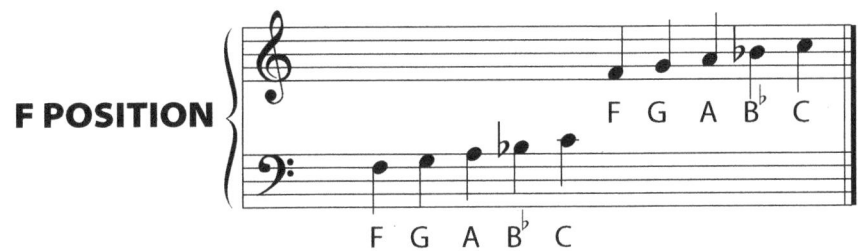

## NOTE NAMING

Name the following notes on the grand staff. Add stems to make them quarter notes.

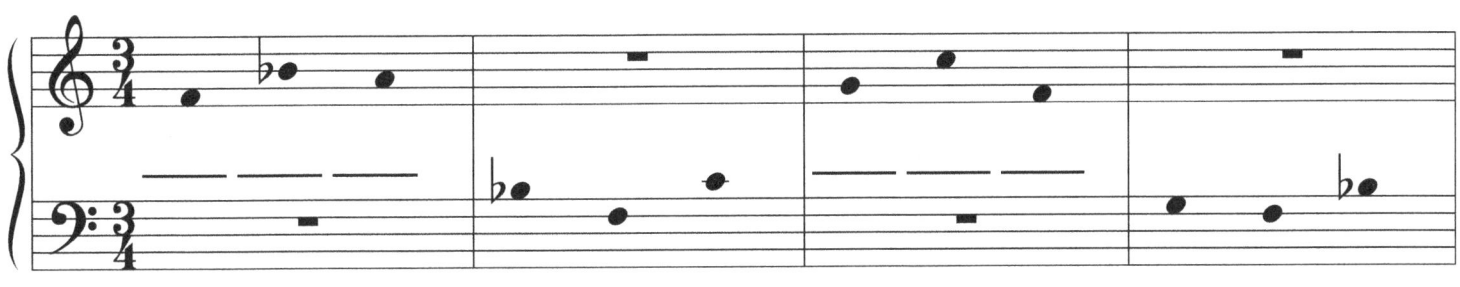

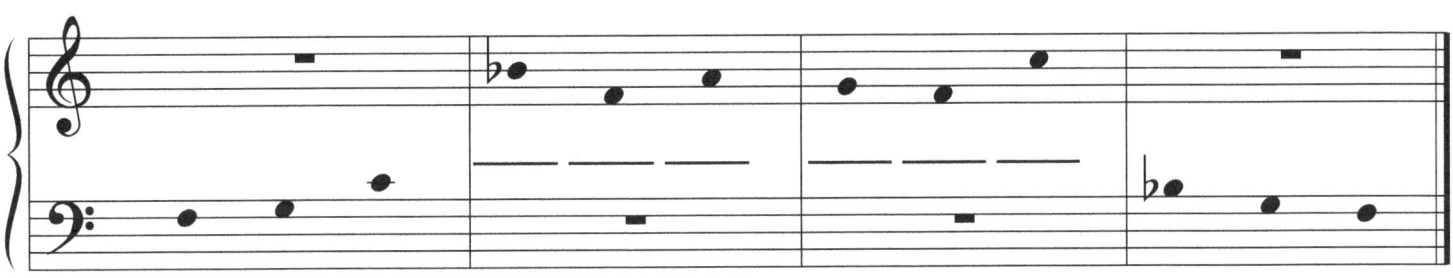

### NOW HEAR THIS!

Your teacher will play a series of short melodies containing eighth notes. Close your eyes and listen. After having heard each melody played twice, clap the rhythm.

### FOR THE TEACHER:

CORRESPONDS WITH PAGE 24 OF BEANSTALK'S LESSON BOOK 1.

# MORE NOTES & STEMS

Add stems where necessary and adjust the note heads to complete the following notes. (Some notes will need to be filled in.)

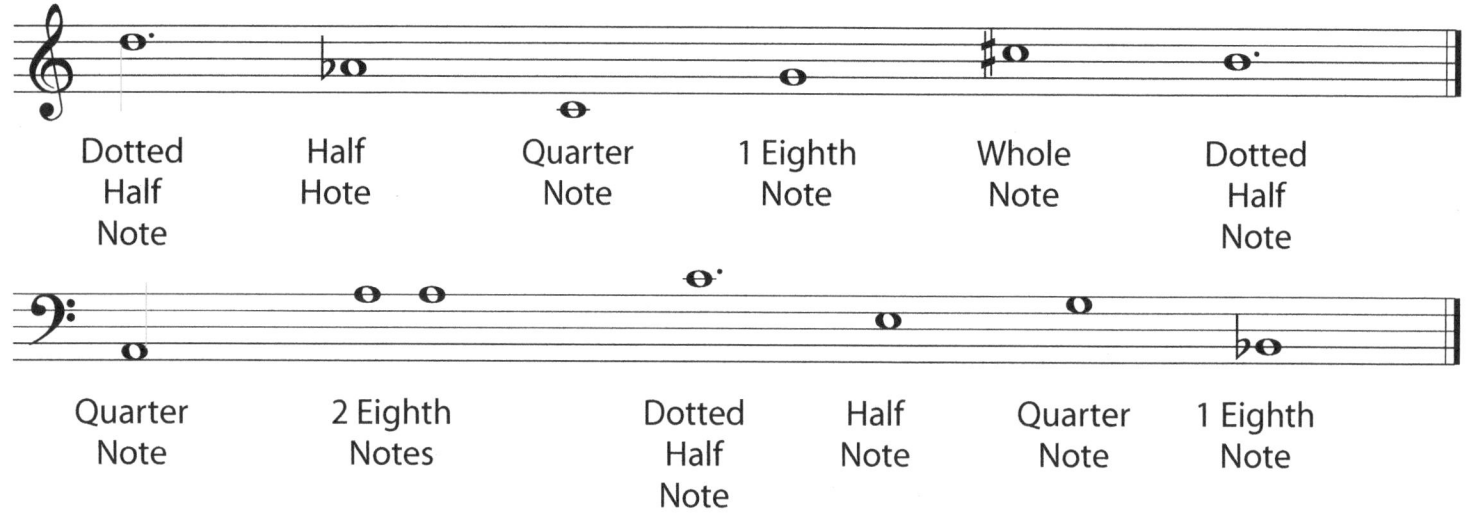

# ADDING BAR LINES

Write the counts and add bar lines to the following. Clap the rhythm and count out loud.

CORRESPONDS WITH PAGE 25 OF BEANSTALK'S LESSON BOOK 1.

# F POSITION TRIAD

Practice writing **F POSITION TRIADS** below.

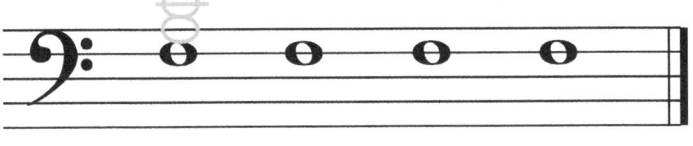

# SECRET MELODY!

1. Add stems.
2. Sight read the following.
3. Name the **SECRET MELODY**!

(TITLE) _____   TRADITIONAL

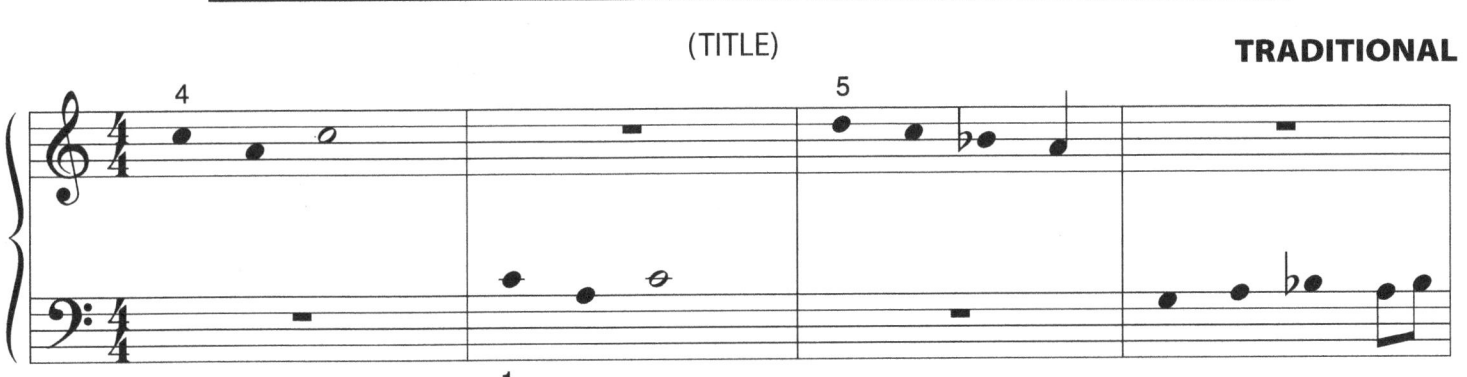

**NOW HEAR THIS!**
Your teacher will play the first few notes from some well known melodies! Close your eyes and listen. Can you name each of the secret melodies?

**FOR THE TEACHER:**

CORRESPONDS WITH PAGE 26 OF BEANSTALK'S LESSON BOOK 1.

# NOTE WRITING

IT'S NICK!

Time yourself writing the following notes on the grand staff. Use dotted half notes.

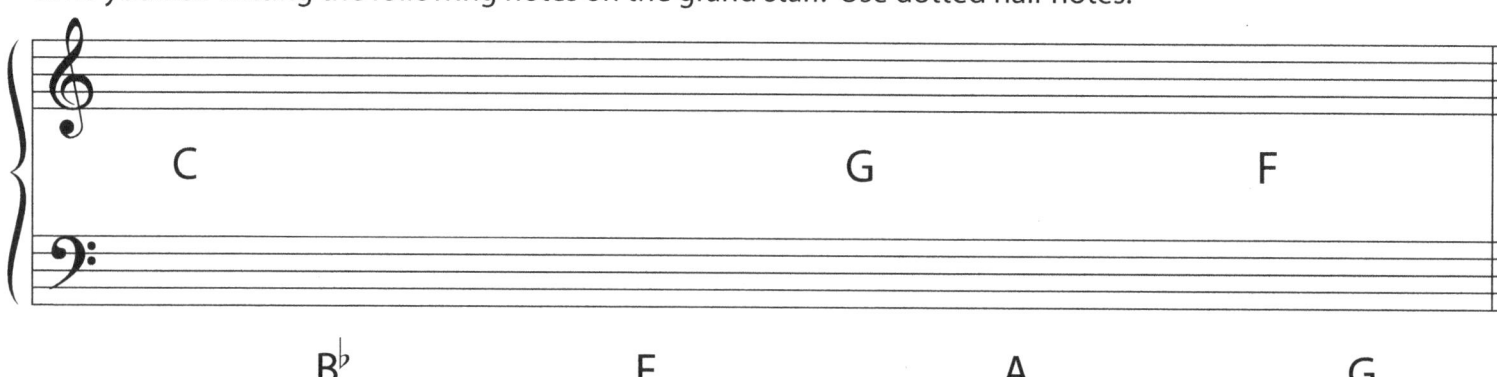

| C | | G | F |
|---|---|---|---|
| B♭ | F | A | G |

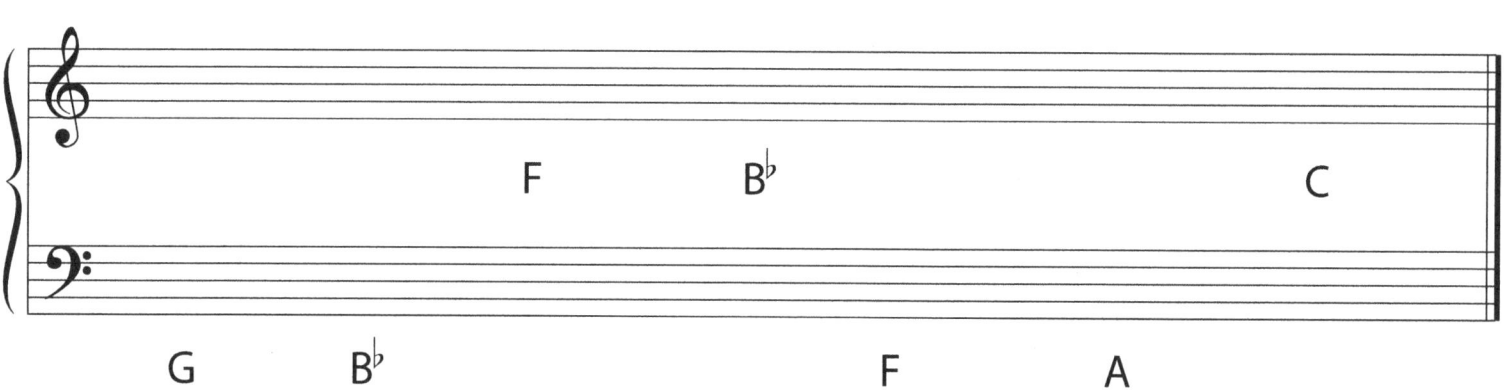

| | F | B♭ | | C |
|---|---|---|---|---|
| G | B♭ | | F | A |

| F | C | G | | B♭ |
|---|---|---|---|---|
| | F | | B♭ | A |

I wrote these notes in _____ minutes and _____ seconds!

CORRESPONDS WITH PAGE 27 OF BEANSTALK'S LESSON BOOK 1.

# D POSITION TRIAD

Practice writing **D POSITION TRIADS** below.

# PUZZLE FUN!

Look at each of the musical signs below. If the sign matches the meaning, color the box **RED**.
If the sign **DOES NOT** match the meaning, color the box **BLUE**.

Can you find the **TIC-TAC-TOE**?

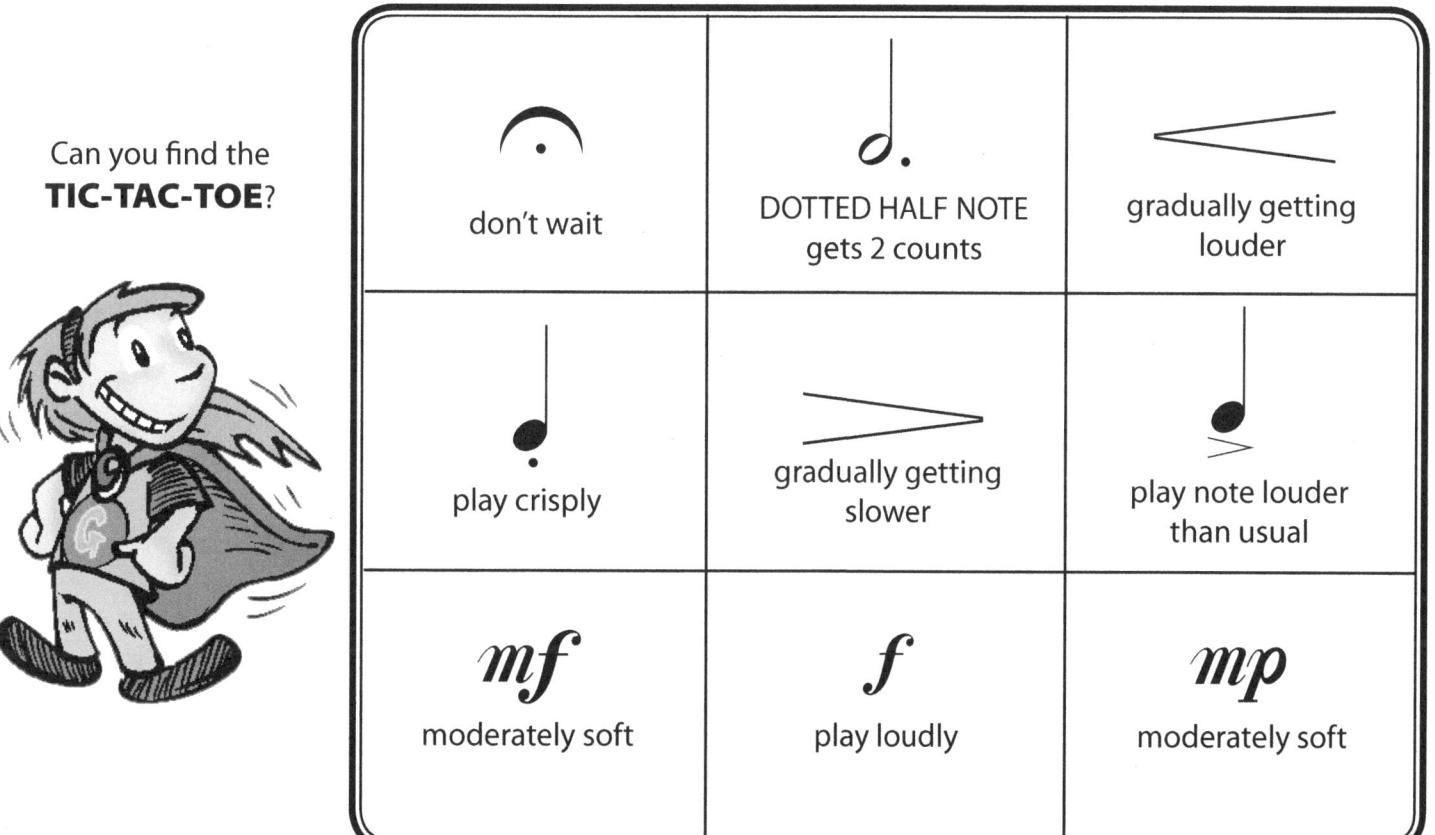

CORRESPONDS WITH PAGE 28 OF BEANSTALK'S LESSON BOOK 1.

# RIDDLES!

I am a sign.
I can sit on a line or in a space.
I tell you to play the next key to the right.
If you touched something like me you'd say ouch!

What am I? _____

Draw me! _____

I am a sign.
I point to the left.
I like to start at a whisper
and and work up to a shout!

What am I? _____

Draw me! _____

I am a sign.
I point to the right.
I like to start at a shout
and end with a whisper!

What am I? _____

Draw me! _____

I am a sign.
I can live above or below a note.
I tell you to play a note louder than usual.
My name is neither French nor Italian.

What am I? _____

Draw me! _____

I am a sign.
I can sit on a line or in a space.
I tell you to play the next key to the left.
Let's hope you don't find one like me on your bike!

What am I? _____

Draw me! _____

I am rather grand.
I help to organize the music.
My 'house' has two 'floors'.
Your right hand lives 'upstairs', your left hand lives 'downstairs'.

What am I? _____

CORRESPONDS WITH PAGE 29 OF BEANSTALK'S LESSON BOOK 1.

# COUNTING & BAR LINES

Write the counts and draw bar lines for the following. Clap the rhythm and count out loud.

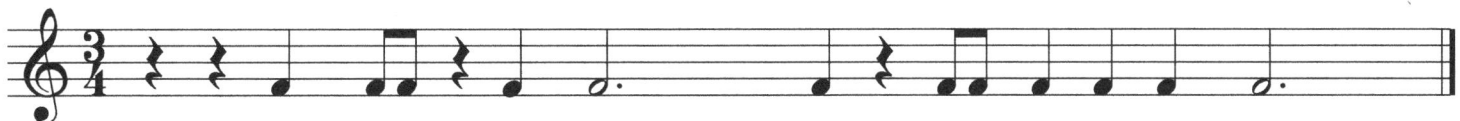

**NOW HEAR THIS!**
Your teacher will play a series of short melodies containing eighth notes. Close your eyes and listen. After having heard each melody played twice, clap the rhythm!

CORRESPONDS WITH PAGES 30 & 31 OF BEANSTALK'S LESSON BOOK 1.

A NEW NOTE: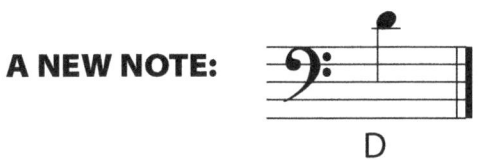

# NOTE NAMING

Name the following notes and add bar lines. (Because these notes are on the grand staff, the bar lines will need to connect the treble and bass clefs.)

CORRESPONDS WITH PAGE 32 OF BEANSTALK'S LESSON BOOK 1.

# REVIEW

1. Name the following notes on the grand staff.

2. Write these notes on the grand staff. Use quarter notes. (Be sure your stems are correct!)

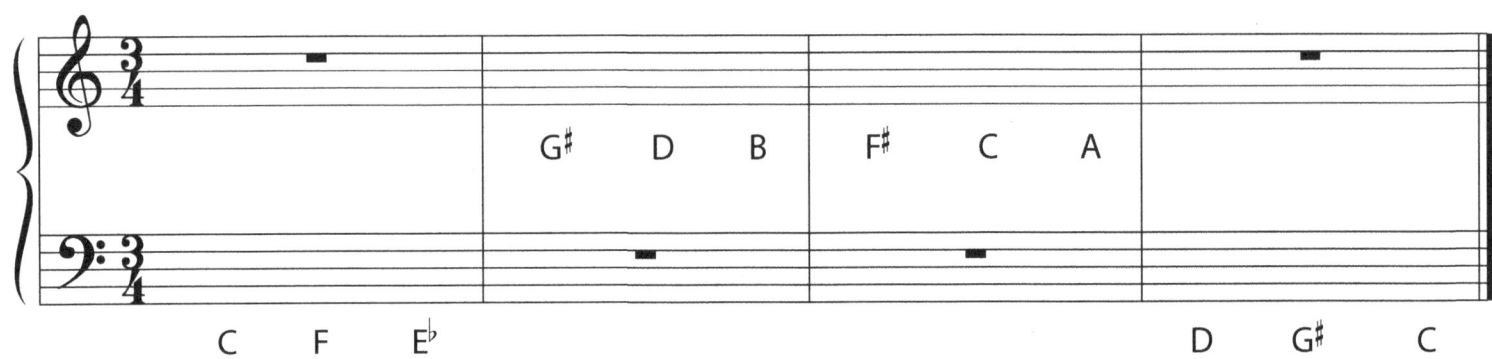

3. Write the counts and add bar lines. Clap the rhythm and count out loud.

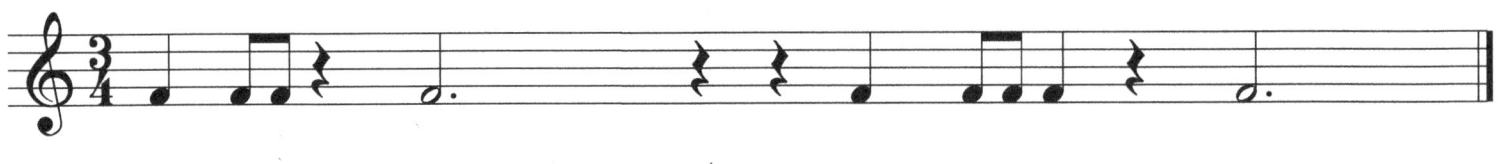

CORRESPONDS WITH PAGE 34 OF BEANSTALK'S LESSON BOOK 1.

4. Add a note above to complete the following **HARMONIC** intervals. Use whole notes.

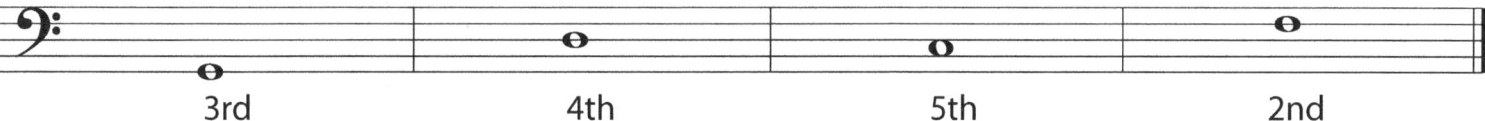

5. Add a note above to complete the following **MELODIC** intervals. Use whole notes.

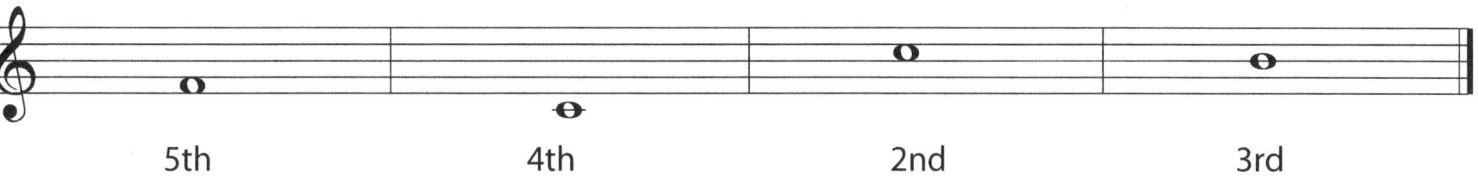

6. Draw a **CIRCLE** around each **SLUR** and a **BOX** around each **TIE**.

7. Add stems where necessary to create the following notes. (You may have to fill in some of the note heads.)

8. Write these triads.

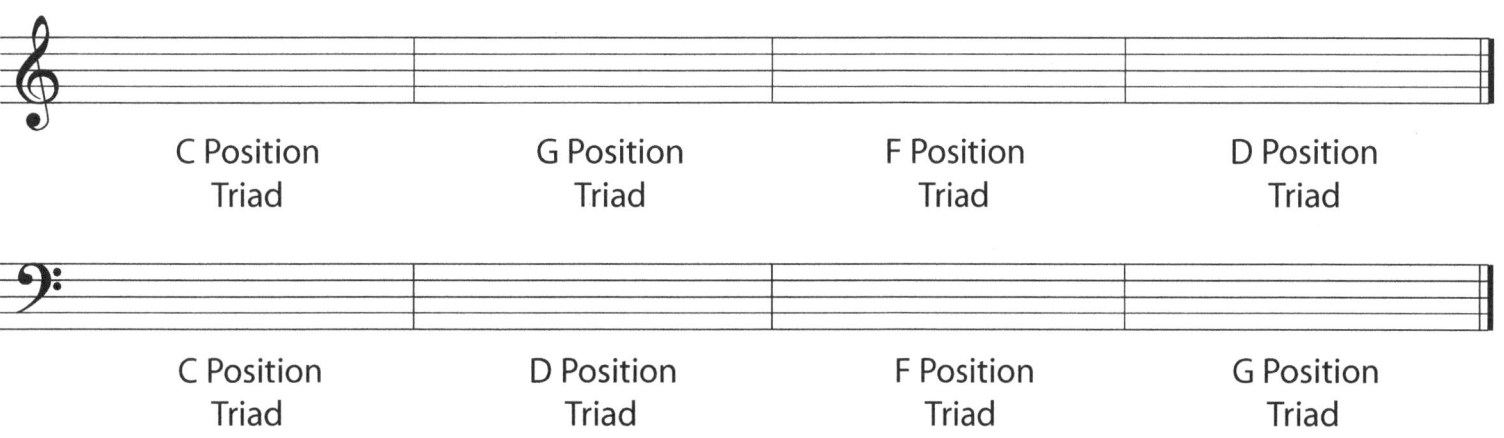

CORRESPONDS WITH PAGE 34 OF BEANSTALK'S LESSON BOOK 1.

# KEY SIGNATURES

A **KEY SIGNATURE** appears at the beginning of the music. It tells us which sharps or flats we must remember to play throughout the piece.

The Key Signature for **C MAJOR** has no **SHARPS** or **FLATS**.

The Key Signature for **G MAJOR** has **F SHARP**.

The Key Signature for **F MAJOR** has **B FLAT**.

Practice writing the key signature for **G MAJOR** on the following grand staffs. The **F SHARP** will always appear on the **TOP LINE** of the **TREBLE CLEF** and on the **4TH LINE** of the **BASS CLEF**.

**THINKING CAP**

How many sharps or flats are there in the key of C major?

Practice writing the key signature for **F MAJOR** on the following grand staffs. The **B FLAT** will always appear on the **MIDDLE LINE** of the **TREBLE CLEF** and on the **2ND LINE** of the **BASS CLEF**.

CORRESPONDS WITH PAGE 35 OF BEANSTALK'S LESSON BOOK 1.

# MORE KEY SIGNATURES!

Color all the **C MAJOR** balloons **RED**.
Color all the **G MAJOR** balloons **GREEN**.
Color all the **F MAJOR** balloons **BLUE**.

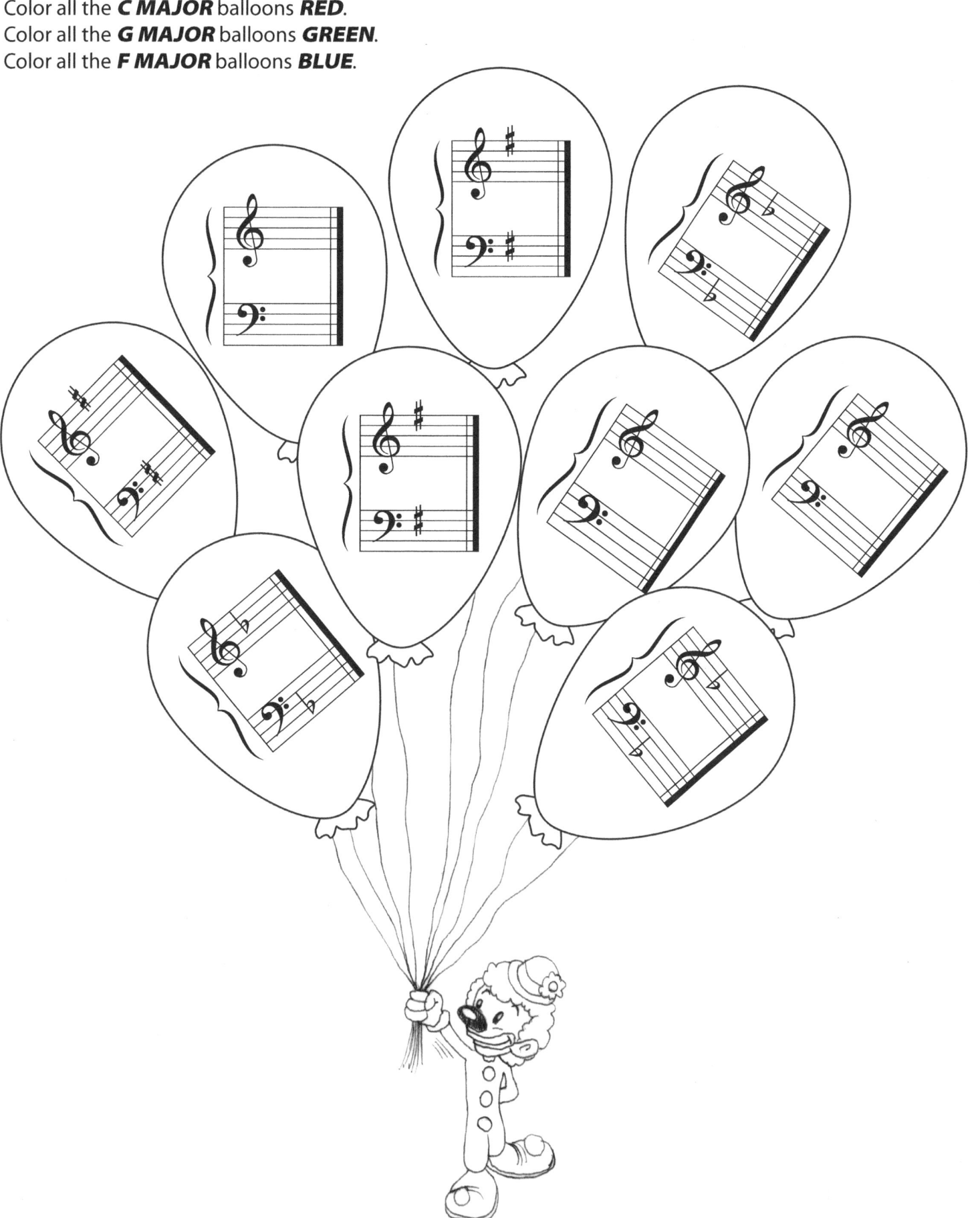

CORRESPONDS WITH PAGE 35 OF BEANSTALK'S LESSON BOOK 1.

# SHARPS

For each line of music below, **CIRCLE** all of the **F SHARPS**. Put the total number of sharps at the end of each line. Which line has the most?

Name the key and sight read each line of music.

SIGHT READING

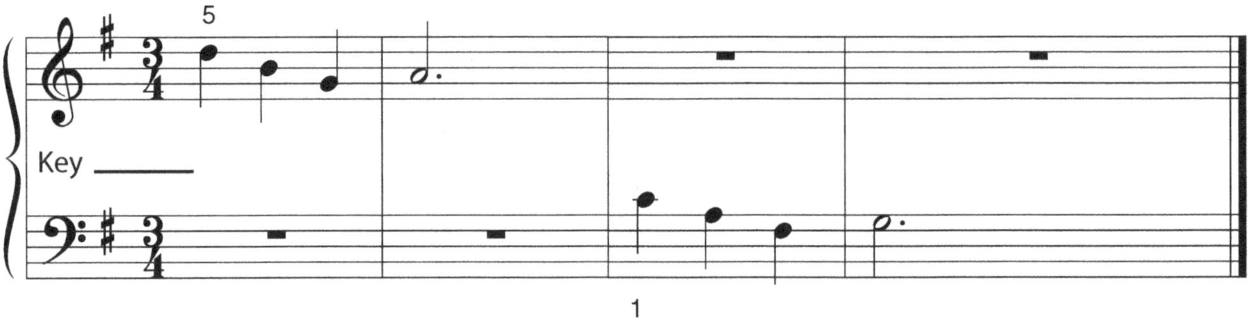

Line 1 has how many #'s?
_____

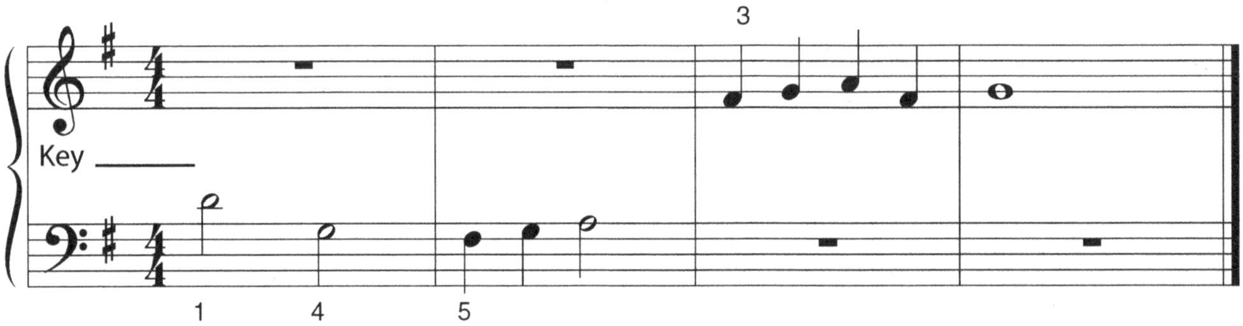

Line 2 has how many #'s?
_____

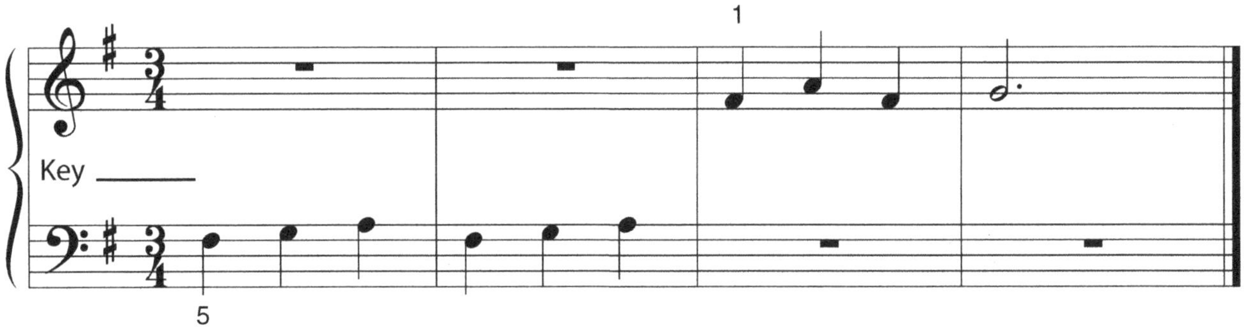

Line 3 has how many #'s?
_____

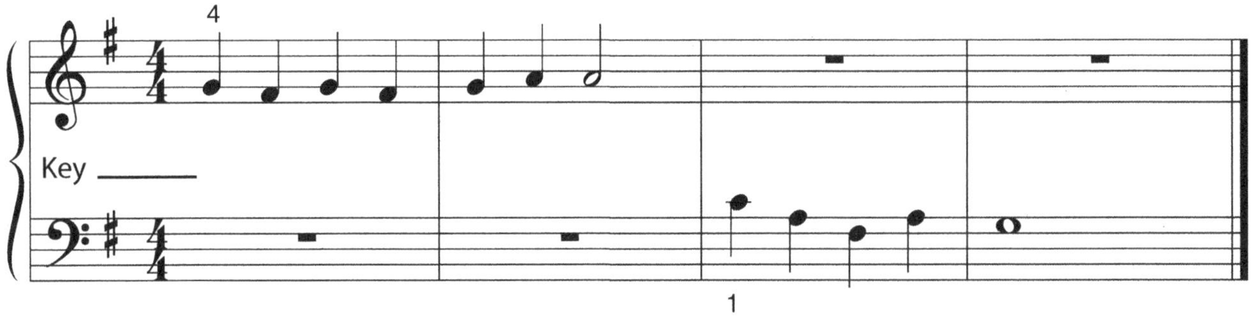

Line 4 has how many #'s?
_____

### THINKING CAP
Which F's do we play as sharp in the key of G major?

The winner is _____!

CORRESPONDS WITH PAGE 36 OF BEANSTALK'S LESSON BOOK 1.

# FLATS

**THINKING CAP**
Which B's do we play as flat in the key of F major?

1. **CIRCLE** all of the **B FLATS** in the following piece of music.
2. Name the key.
3. Sight read the piece. Do you recognize the melody?
4. Fill in the title on the line provided.

_____
(TITLE)

**TRADITIONAL**

CORRESPONDS WITH PAGE 37 OF BEANSTALK'S LESSON BOOK 1.

# HOW'S YOUR ITALIAN?

**TEMPO** means rate of speed. Most tempo markings used in music are written in **ITALIAN**.

Here are some common Italian tempo markings and their meanings:

**MODERATO** tells us to play at a **MODERATE** speed.

**ALLEGRO** means **QUICK** and **LIVELY**.

**THINKING CAP**
Name an activity that you do at each one of these speeds.

**RITARDANDO** means to **GRADUALLY GET SLOWER**.

**LENTO** means to play **SLOWLY**.

**ANDANTE** means to play **RATHER SLOWLY** or at a **WALKING PACE**.

**CIRCLE** these hidden Italian terms in the puzzle below. The words may be written down or across. (**TEMPO** has been done for you as an example.)

~~TEMPO~~          **MODERATO**          **ALLEGRO**
**RITARDANDO**     **LENTO**             **ANDANTE**

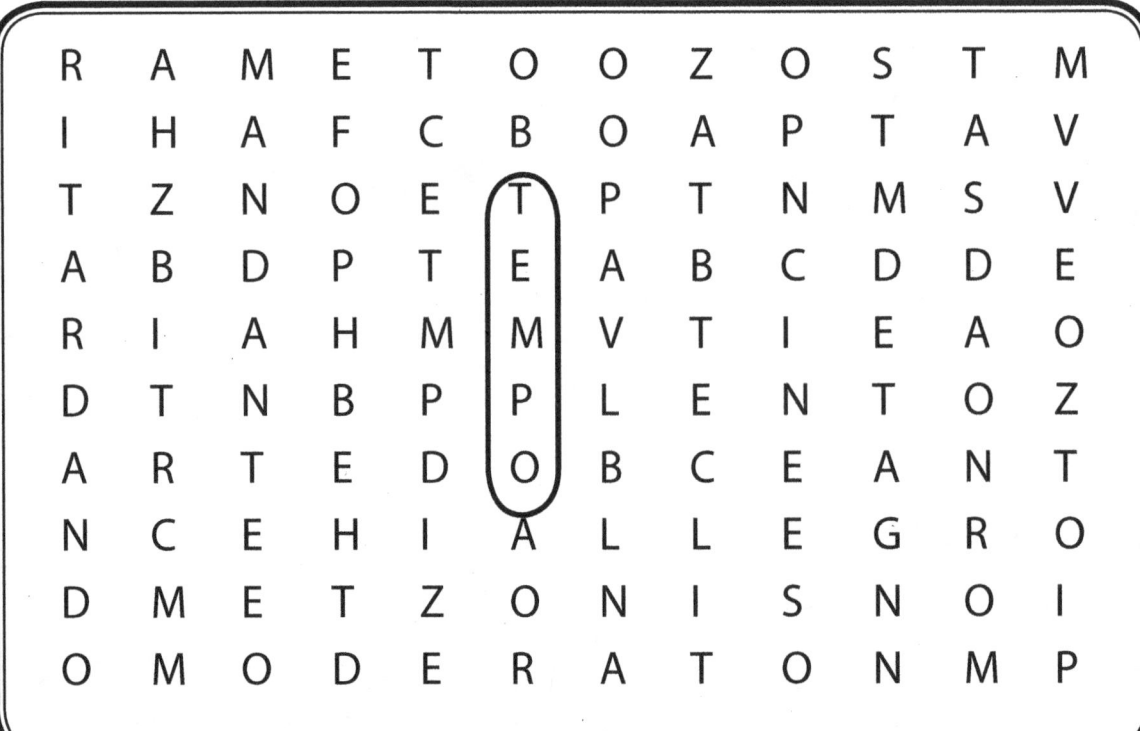

CORRESPONDS WITH PAGE 38 OF BEANSTALK'S LESSON BOOK 1.

# COMPOSE IT!

Finally it's your turn! You get to compose your own piece!

Below you will find **EIGHT** measures. Using the notes of **C POSITION (C D E F G)** finish the composition! The only rules to remember are that you must have **FOUR** beats (or counts) in each measure and that you must have **FUN** being a composer!

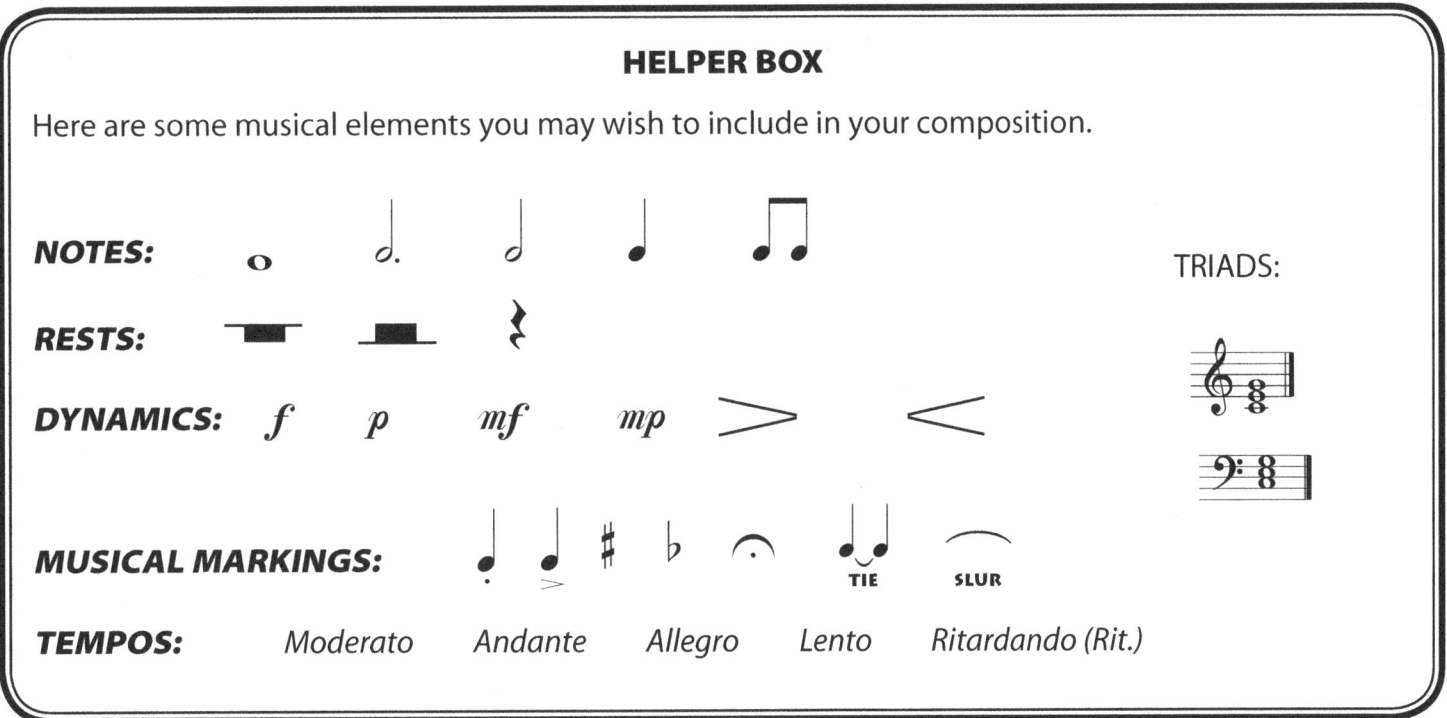

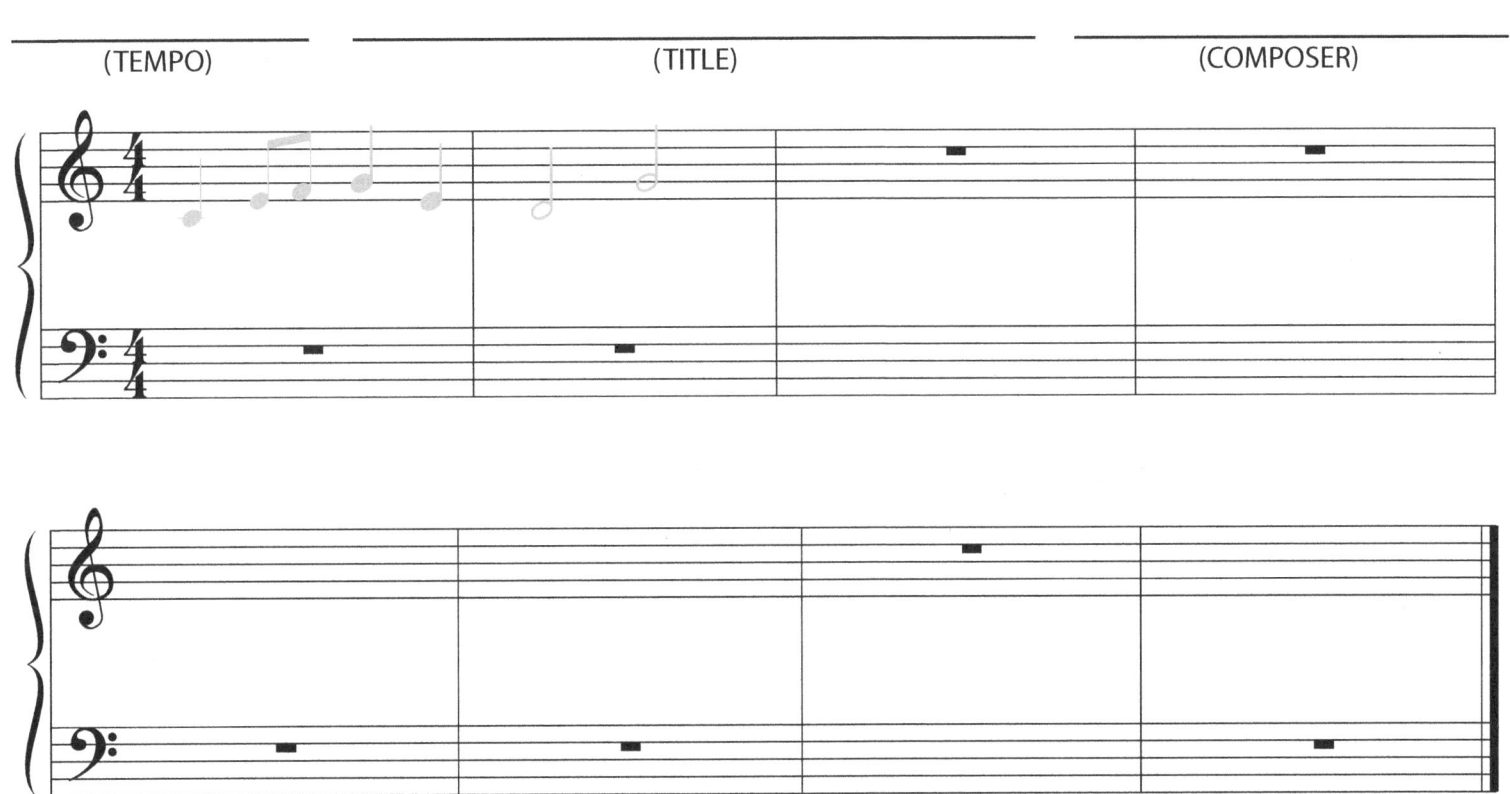

CORRESPONDS WITH PAGE 39 OF BEANSTALK'S LESSON BOOK 1.

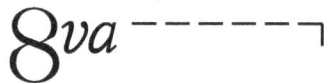

# OCTAVE HIGHER

The 8va sign **ABOVE** the music means that all the notes are to be played an **OCTAVE HIGHER** than written. For example, an octave higher than **MIDDLE C** is the next **C** above.

How it is written:

Where it is actually played:

Play the following melody. **CIRCLE** each group of three notes which is to be played an **OCTAVE HIGHER**.

For the following notes, write the note which is an **OCTAVE HIGHER**. (The first one has been done for you as an example.)

CORRESPONDS WITH PAGE 40 OF BEANSTALK'S LESSON BOOK 1.

# OCTAVE LOWER

The *8va* sign **BELOW** the music means that all the notes are to be played an **OCTAVE LOWER** than written. For example, an octave lower than **MIDDLE C** is the next **C** below.

How it is written:

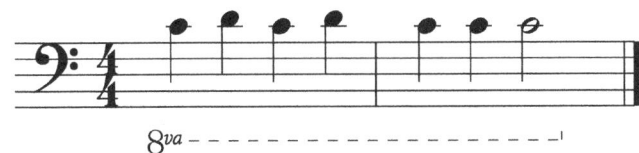

Where it is actually played:

Play the following melody. **CIRCLE** each group of notes which is to be played an **OCTAVE HIGHER**. Draw a **BOX** around each group of notes which is to be played an **OCTAVE LOWER**.

**TRADITIONAL**

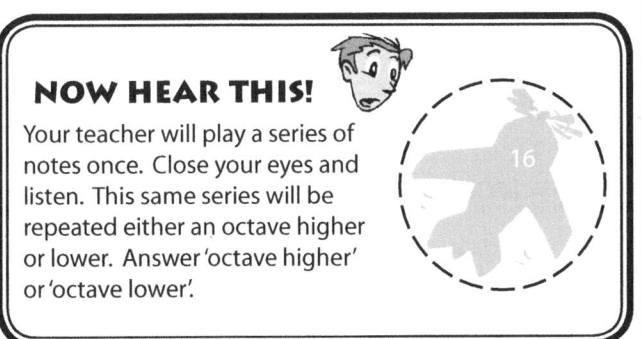

### NOW HEAR THIS!
Your teacher will play a series of notes once. Close your eyes and listen. This same series will be repeated either an octave higher or lower. Answer 'octave higher' or 'octave lower'.

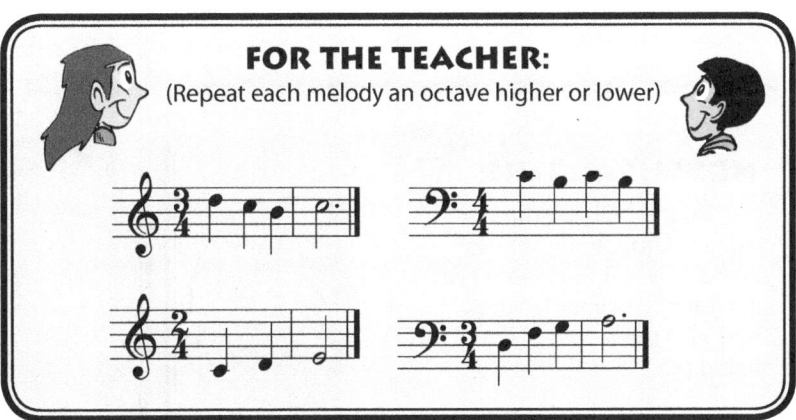

### FOR THE TEACHER:
(Repeat each melody an octave higher or lower)

CORRESPONDS WITH PAGES 41 & 42 OF BEANSTALK'S LESSON BOOK 1.

# SECRET MELODY!

1. Add stems.
2. Sight read the following.
3. Name the **SECRET MELODY**!
4. Fill in the note names.

_____
(TITLE)

**TRADITIONAL**

[musical score]

### NOW HEAR THIS!
Your teacher will play the first few notes from some famous melodies twice! Close your eyes and listen. Can you clap the rhythm of the secret melodies?

**FOR THE TEACHER:**

**CORRESPONDS WITH PAGE 42 OF BEANSTALK'S LESSON BOOK 1.**

# RIDDLES!

I am a sign.
I am not quite soft.
My closest friend is **PIANO**.
My first name is **MEZZO**.

What am I? _____

Draw me! _____

I am a sign.
I can sit above or below a note.
When you see me you must stop and wait.
My English name rhymes with 'cause'.

What am I? _____

Draw me! _____

I can have sharps.
I can have flats.
I can have neither sharps or flats.
My 'signature' appears at the beginning
of a piece of music.

What am I? _____

I am a note.
My stem has a flag.
Sometimes I like to hold hands
with others just like me.
When there are **TWO** of us
together, we get **ONE** count.

What am I? _____

Draw me! _____

I am a ruler.
I measure distance.
Some say I look melodic.
Some say I look harmonic.

What am I? _____

Draw one of me!

I am a sign.
I am closer to loud than soft.
My closest friend is **FORTE**.
My first name is **MEZZO**.

What am I? _____

Draw me! _____

CORRESPONDS WITH PAGE 42 OF BEANSTALK'S LESSON BOOK 1.

# NOTE NAMING

IT'S NICK!

Time yourself naming the following notes on the grand staff. Be sure to check the key signature!

1.

I named these notes in _____ minutes and _____ seconds!

2.

I named these notes in _____ minutes and _____ seconds!

CORRESPONDS WITH PAGES 43 & 44 OF BEANSTALK'S LESSON BOOK 1.

# PUZZLE FUN!
## YOU BE THE TEACHER!

This is Melody's homework. Find out if she did a good job! Read each question carefully and then read Melody's answers. Put a (✓) check mark if she answered correctly or an (✗) if she answered incorrectly. If her answer was incorrect, write the correct answer on the line provided.

|   | Melody's Answers | ✓ or ✗ | Your correction if necessary |
|---|---|---|---|
| 1. Draw a sign which tells us to play **LOUDLY**. | *f* | | |
| 2. Draw an interval of a 4th. Make it **HARMONIC**. | [bass clef with notes] | | [bass clef] |
| 3. Draw a sign which tells us to play **GRADUALLY SOFTER**. | < | | |
| 4. Draw a sign which tells us to play **MODERATELY SOFT**. | *p* | | |
| 5. Draw a **SHARP** sign in the correct position in front of this note. | [treble clef with ♯ note] | | [treble clef with note] |
| 6. Draw a **FLAT** sign in the correct position in front of this note. | [treble clef with ♭ note] | | [treble clef with note] |
| 7. Draw a sign over this note that tells us to **HOLD** longer than its usual value. | [bass clef with > over note] | | [bass clef] |
| 8. Draw a sign that tells us to play **GRADUALLY LOUDER**. | > | | |

CORRESPONDS WITH PAGES 45 & 46 OF BEANSTALK'S LESSON BOOK 1.

# COUNTING & BAR LINES

Write the counts and add bar lines to the following. Clap the rhythm and count out loud.

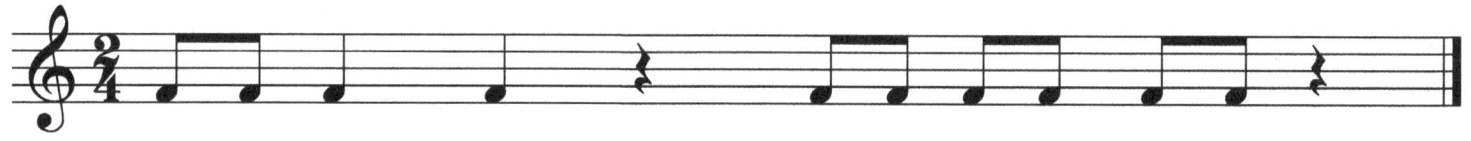

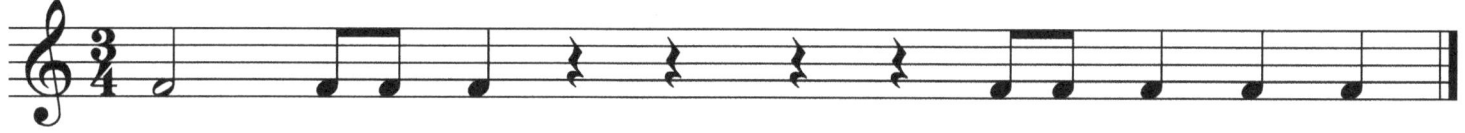

CORRESPONDS WITH PAGE 46 OF BEANSTALK'S LESSON BOOK 1.

# NATURALS

A **NATURAL** cancels a sharp or flat.
When we write a natural sign, we place it **IN FRONT** of the note.

If the natural is going in front of a **SPACE** note, the sign must go in the **SPACE**:

Practice writing **NATURAL** signs in front of these **SPACE** notes.

**DRAWING REMINDER**: to draw a **NATURAL** sign, first write the letter 'L' and then the number '7'.

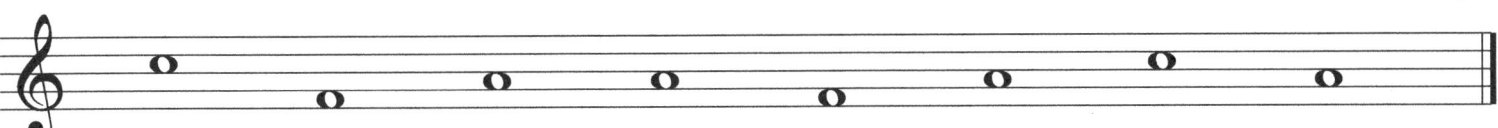

If the natural is going in front of a **LINE** note, the sign must go on the **LINE**:

Practice writing **NATURAL** signs in front of these **LINE** notes.

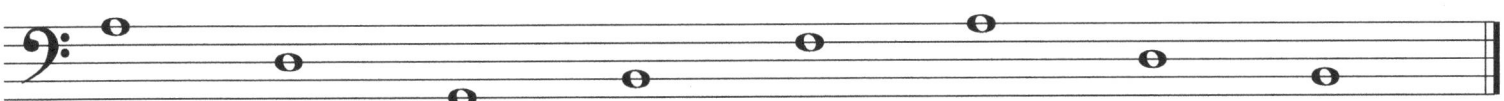

Name the following notes. Remember, if the note has a sharp or a flat sign, that same note will remain a sharp or flat for the **ENTIRE** measure unless it is cancelled by a natural.

B♭  B♮  B♮

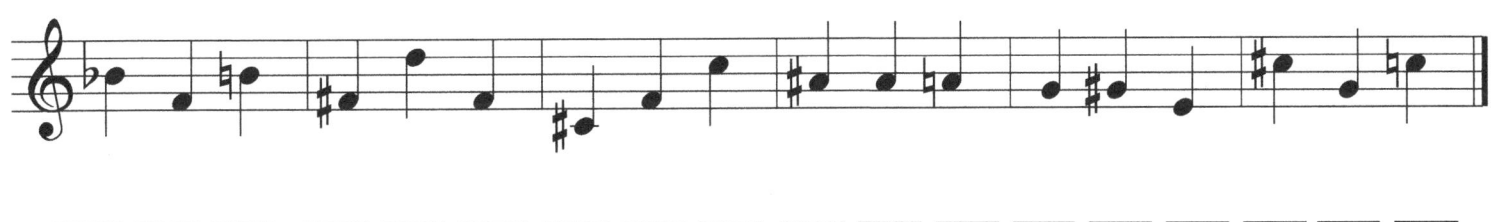

CORRESPONDS WITH PAGE 47 OF BEANSTALK'S LESSON BOOK 1.

45

# NOTE WRITING

IT'S NICK!

Time yourself writing the following notes on the grand staff. Use quarter notes. (Remember to check the key signature!)

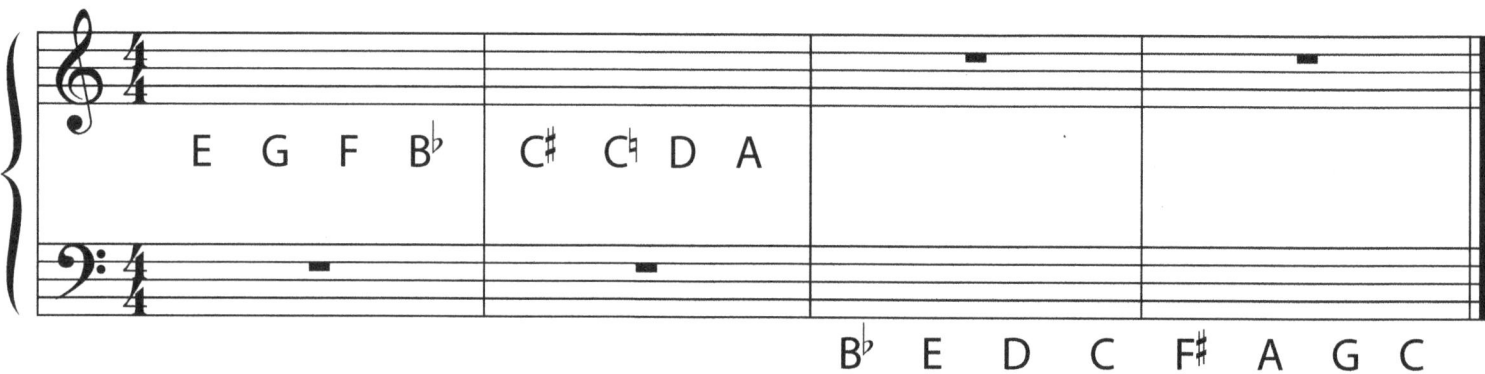

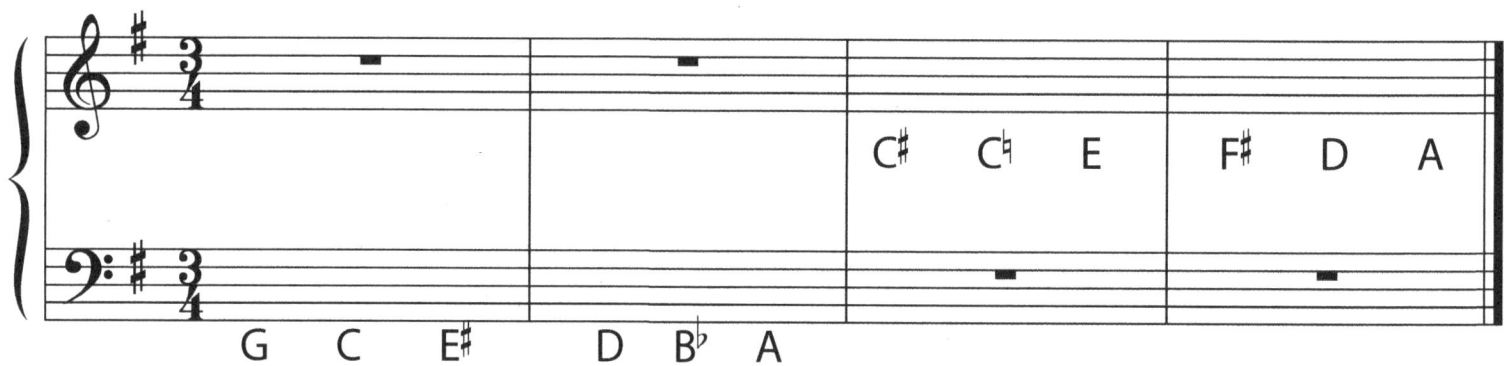

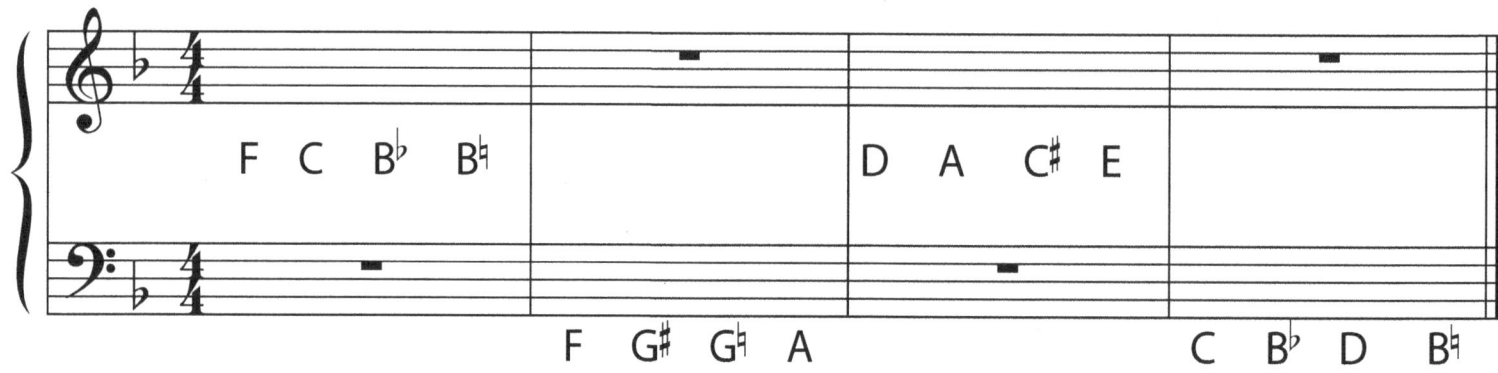

I wrote these notes in _____ minutes and _____ seconds!

CORRESPONDS WITH PAGE 48 OF BEANSTALK'S LESSON BOOK 1.

# REVIEW

1. Name the following notes on the grand staff. Make each note **STACCATO**.

2. Write the following notes on the grand staff. Use quarter notes.

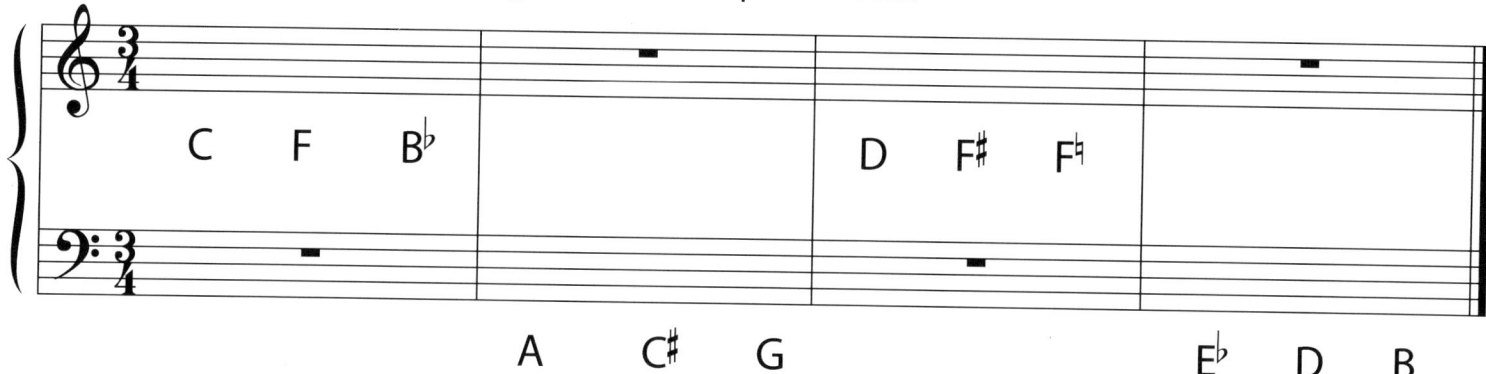

3. Write the counts and add bar lines to the following. Clap the rhythm and count out loud.

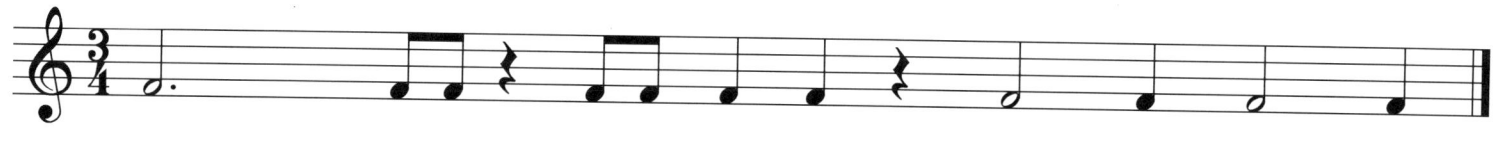

4. Add a note above to complete each of the following **MELODIC** intervals. Use whole notes.

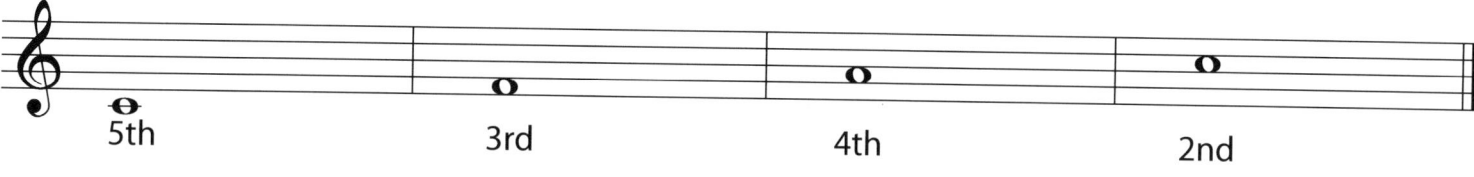

CORRESPONDS WITH PAGE 49 & 50 OF BEANSTALK'S LESSON BOOK 1.

5. Write the following triads. Use whole notes.

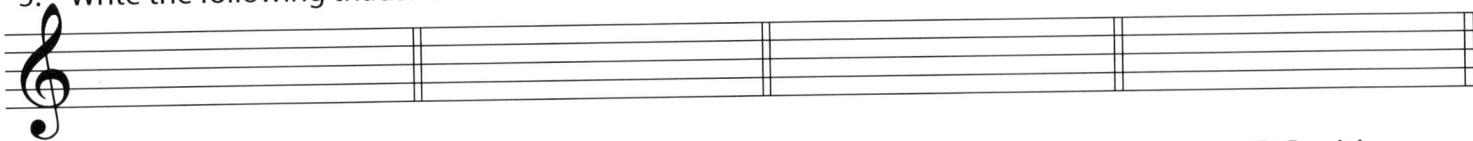

C Position        G Position        F Position        D Position

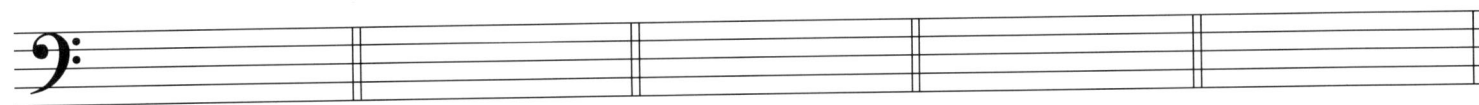

C Position     G Position     F Position     D Position     G Position

6. Write the following key signatures.

Key of G Major

Key of F Major

7. Connect the opposites by drawing a line.

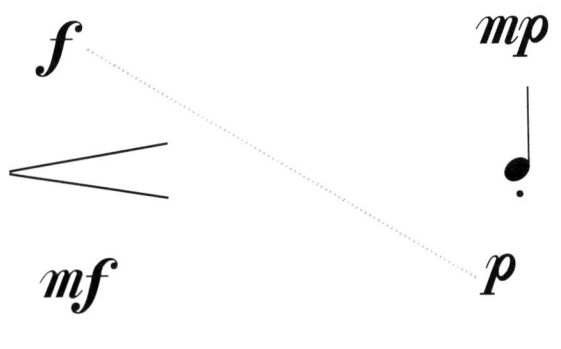

8. Match the following to their meaning by drawing a line.

| | |
|---|---|
| **ANDANTE** | play the note louder than usual |
| **RITARDANDO** | play slowly |
| **LENTO** | rate of speed |
| **ALLEGRO** | play slowly and at a walking pace |
| **TEMPO** | play at a moderate speed |
| ♩ | gradually getting slower |
| > | quick and lively |
| **MODERATO** | |

CORRESPONDS WITH PAGE 49 & 50 OF BEANSTALK'S LESSON BOOK 1.